formatio

TRADITION. EXPERIENCE.
TRANSFORMATION.

Formatio books from InterVarsity Press follow the rich tradition of the church in the journey of spiritual formation. These books are not merely about being informed, but about being transformed by Christ and conformed to his image. Formatio stands in InterVarsity Press's evangelical publishing tradition by integrating God's Word with spiritual practice and by prompting readers to move from inward change to outward witness. InterVarsity Press uses the chambered nautilus for Formatio, a symbol of spiritual formation because of its continual spiral journey outward as it moves from its center. We believe that each of us is made with a deep desire to be in God's presence. Formatio books help us to fulfill our deepest desires and to become our true selves in light of God's grace.

james Bryan smith

The Good and Beautiful
COMMUNITY

FOLLOWING THE SPIRIT,

EXTENDING GRACE,

DEMONSTRATING LOVE

IVP Books

An imprint of InterVarsity Press
Downers Grove, Illinois

InterVarsity Press
P.O. Box 1400, Downers Grove, IL 60515-1426
www.ivpress.com
email@ivpress.com

InterVarsity Press® is the book-publishing division of InterVarsity Christian Fellowship/USA®, a movement of students and faculty active on campus at hundreds of universities, colleges and schools of nursing in the United States of America, and a member movement of the International Fellowship of Evangelical Students. For information about local and regional activities, visit intervarsity.org.

All Scripture quotations, unless otherwise indicated, are taken from the New Revised Standard Version of the Bible, copyright 1989 by Division of Christian Education of the National Council of the Churches of Christ in the USA. Used by permission. All rights reserved.

Design: Cindy Kiple
Images: © Marcin Smirnow/iStockphoto

ISBN 978-0-8308-3533-1

Printed in Canada ∞

Library of Congress Cataloging-in-Publication Data

Smith, James Bryan.
  The good and beautiful community: following the spirit, extending
grace, demonstrating love/James Bryan Smith.
     p. cm.—(The apprentice series)
  Includes bibliographical references.
  ISBN 978-0-8308-3533-1 (cloth: alk. paper)
  1. Communities—Religious aspects—Christianity. 2. Christian life.
1. Title.
  BV625.S65 2010
  262—dc22

                                                                      2010014229

P   27   26   25   24   23   22   21   20   19   18   17   16   15   14   13   12   11   10
Y   35   34   33   32   31   30   29   28   27   26   25   24   23   22   21   20   19   18

For my good and beautiful community:

Meghan Smith, Matt Johnson, Catherine Johnson,

Janeen Sehl, Patrick Sehl, Laura Fox, C. J. Fox,

Jimmy Taylor and Andrew Tash

For standing with me,
heart and soul

1 SAMUEL 14:7 NIV

contents

introduction

The Apprentice Series is designed to help people in their efforts to grow in Christlikeness. The series is built on a basic formula for transformation that includes a mental side (changing narratives), a physical side (practicing spiritual exercises), a communal side (doing the first two in the context of community) and a spiritual side (the work of the Holy Spirit). I have come to believe that real transformation must be holistic, taking into account the many dimensions of human life.

Five years of field-testing this material has taught me a lot about how we change and what things impede us. What I discovered is that when people engage in all three of these activities—under the leading of the Spirit—transformation is not only possible but also practically inevitable. Every person who really applied him- or herself to this curriculum experienced noticeable change. Their friends and spouses noticed and soon signed up to try it for themselves.

THE FIRST TWO BOOKS
The three core books of The Apprentice Series follow a logical progression. The first book, *The Good and Beautiful God*, deals with our

"God narratives," or our thoughts about God. The premise is that our thoughts about God must be aligned with Jesus or we will be starting in the wrong direction, and our life with God will be negatively affected, perhaps even toxic. Once people have "fallen in love with the God Jesus knows," they are ready to take a look in the mirror and examine their own soul. That is the aim of the second book, *The Good and Beautiful Life*. It deals primarily with character and virtue. Following Jesus' teaching in the Sermon on the Mount, the book addresses common struggles in human life, such as anger, lust, lying, worry and judging others.

Each chapter of these books follows a similar pattern. Through real-life stories the reader is invited to examine the false ideas and narratives that hinder our lives, and then replace them with the true narratives found in Jesus' teaching and the rest of the Bible. Each chapter also includes a soul-training exercise that is chosen specifically to help with the narrative change. You can simply read the book, and nothing more, and perhaps experience some gain. Or you can read a chapter and practice the exercise, and experience a little more change. Best of all, however, is reading the chapter reflectively, engaging in the exercise wholeheartedly, and discussing your experiences and insights with a group of fellow travelers on the journey. This last way has proven the most effective.

HEART, GRACE AND ACTION

In addition to the basic formula for transformation (narrative, exercise, community—Holy Spirit), this three-book curriculum also teaches some basic principles that are crucial aspects of Christian spiritual formation. These have been important in the first two books and are even more important in this book, which deals more directly with how we live, not just our love for God (the first book) or curing our own souls (book two). In *The Good and Beautiful Community* we are going to examine the second part of the Great Commandment: loving our neighbor as ourselves.

When we move into this area, it is easy to lose the main focus (the heart) and put all of the emphasis on the wrong thing (the activity itself). Paul understood this so well when he wrote to the Corinthians, "If I give away all I have, and if I deliver up my body to be burned, but have not love, I gain nothing" (1 Corinthians 13:3 ESV).

We can engage in the highest acts of service and martyrdom, but if we do not do it in a spirit of love, it is of no value. When we deal with social justice, acts of mercy or serving others, there is a tendency to become enamored with the action itself. Serving others is rare and impressive in our narcissistic world, a world where people create little cocoons and isolate themselves from others, often out of fear. When we see people sacrificing their time or money for others, it gains our attention. There is nothing wrong with this. We must not—indeed cannot—hide our light under a bushel. But we must beware; our good works can also lead to vainglory (discussed in the second book). Instead of our works glorifying our Father who is in heaven, we do things to glorify ourselves on earth.

The same can be said of our personal piety. It is easy to turn prayer or Bible reading into ways we establish our merit with God and others. Jesus criticized the Pharisees, not for engaging in prayer, fasting and almsgiving, but for practicing them simply to be "seen by others" (Matthew 6:5). A favorite phrase I often use is, "The heart of the matter is the matter of the heart."

With that caveat in place, let me say clearly that while this is a problem, it is not the primary problem. The main failure in our lives as Christians is our comparative lack of good works. Many—myself included, at one time—have been led to believe that we are saved by faith alone and not by our works, as if our works are unnecessary. Many love to quote Ephesians 2:8-9 to state this point. While it is true that our works do not—cannot—save us, it is also true that we were created to do good works. All we need to do is read verse 10. Let's look at all three verses:

For by grace you have been saved through faith, and this is not your own doing; it is the gift of God—not the result of works, so that no one may boast. For we are what he has made us, created in Christ Jesus for good works, which God prepared beforehand to be our way of life. (Ephesians 2:8-10)

If we read all three verses, we reach the right balance: Grace (God's action in our lives) is accessed by faith (trust and confidence), and we enter into a relationship of love. We know that God loves us, and we love God in return (1 John 4:10).

That is not the end of the story but the beginning of a new way of living. That love can and must extend itself through our hands and feet, expressed in our love for others. We were created for a purpose. Not simply to wait until we die and go to heaven, but created "in Christ Jesus for good works." Faith and works are not opposed; faith ought to lead to works, and indeed, works are a natural outgrowth of faith. James makes this point clearly:

What good is it, my brothers and sisters, if you say you have faith but do not have works? Can faith save you? If a brother or sister is naked and lacks daily food, and one of you says to them, "Go in peace; keep warm and eat your fill," and yet you do not supply their bodily needs, what is the good of that? So faith by itself, if it has no works, is dead. (James 2:14-17)

But what kind of faith is James talking about?

PERSONAL PIETY AND SOCIAL ACTION

There are two kinds of faith: dead faith and living faith. Dead faith is personal piety or doctrinal orthodoxy. There is faith, to be sure, faith in one's own practices or dogma. But it is dead faith. It breeds no life. It is like the Dead Sea, from which nothing flows out, and thus it has no life in it. Living faith is faith working through love. According to Paul, this is the only thing that matters: "The only thing that counts is faith working through love" (Galatians 5:6). Living faith is trust and confidence in God expressed in acts of love in our human relations and encounters with one another.

So far I have tried to steer clear of two common errors: (1) focusing on the act itself and (2) focusing on personal faith. The former is common in circles where social action is the primary concern. The latter is common among those who stress personal faith or piety. I have noticed that quite often these two aspects are completely divorced from one another. People who stress social justice sometimes do so with little or no emphasis on personal piety; people who stress personal piety often fail to practice social justice with consistency and regularity. In this book I want to wed these two essential aspects of being an apprentice of Jesus.

Social action without personal piety can easily become self-righteous and insensitive and lead to burnout. Personal piety without social action can also become self-righteous and insensitive and lead to burnout. The problems are, ironically, identical. Both tend to see their actions (service or prayer) as the way to earn the favor of God and humans. Both can be insensitive to others (activists who force their kindness on people who are not ready for it; pietists who are insensitive to the needs of others). And both lead to burnout because they are not empowered by the Spirit, only by the flesh.

So the aim here is to create a happy marriage between contemplation and action, piety and mercy, personal devotion and social service. As I said, this is not common, but it has been evident in all of the great movements in Christian history. Saint Francis spent hours in contemplation, yet he also cared for the poor, the sick and the outcast. John Wesley told the Methodists that "acts of piety and works of mercy" were two essential sides of the same coin. The early Methodists were known for their personal as well as social holiness. Wesley would not allow either aspect to be neglected.

THE TRUE SOCIAL ACTIVIST
Dallas Willard and I were once talking about social justice and community service. He asked me, "Jim, who is the true social activist?"

I thought of people like Mother Teresa, who served unselfishly among the poor in Calcutta, or perhaps Martin Luther King Jr., who fought against injustice in a loving way. Unsure, I simply said, "I don't know, who?" His answer was surprising: "The true social activist is the person who lives as an apprentice of Jesus in his or her ordinary relationships." He went on to say that social activism is not an act but a way of being. We are prone, he said, to put the emphasis on the action—serving, protesting, refusing to comply—but in fact the emphasis should first be on the heart or character.

Then Dr. Willard went on to explain that every relationship, and every action, would be affected by our apprenticeship. It is not that we do a good deed here and there, but that our very lives are good deeds. The character of Christ that is infused in us will be a part of every encounter. The fact that an apprentice tells the truth will affect his or her entire workplace. The fact that an apprentice of Jesus is not ruled by fear or greed will make a difference at home and in his or her communities. I liked how Dallas shifted the focus from the act to the heart, from the exterior to the interior. Too often people engage in social action on a part-time basis—a visit to the soup kitchen, a short-term mission trip—and feel that they have done more than their share in the area of service.

While those are good activities, if they do not flow from a Christlike character, they are merely temporary acts of kindness. Apprentices of Jesus are not part-time do-gooders. They live in continuous contact with the kingdom of God and are constantly men and women in whom Christ dwells. They do not sometimes tell the truth, sometimes live sacrificially or sometimes forgive. There are myriad opportunities for us to affect the world we live in. That is why this book will try to examine the many ways we relate to others and what that might mean for those who live with Christ in his available kingdom.

ONE IN WHOM CHRIST DWELLS
As in the first two books, the essential narratives for an apprentice

have to do with identity and location. As Christ-followers we are people in whom Christ dwells. This is our fundamental identity. It is not up for grabs; it is not subject to change, regardless of our behavior. The essential idea here is that our identity should shape our behavior, but we live in a world where that is reversed: behavior determines identity in this world. But we do not belong to this world. It is not our home. We set our hearts and minds on another world (Colossians 3:1-2). I recently was awakened to a beautiful phrase that describes our truest identity. It comes from Eugene Peterson, who notes that we are a "splendid, never-to-be-duplicated story of grace."

As a person Christ dwells in and delights in, as a splendid story of grace, I am sacred, set apart for God, special and empowered by the same power that raised Jesus from the dead (Romans 6:3-4). I am sacred and I am strong, and I can do all things through Christ who strengthens me (Philippians 4:13). Greater is he that is in me than he that is in the world (1 John 4:4). This awareness is essential for those who are striving to live as apprentices of Jesus in a world that has rejected Jesus and his values. But there is more good news. Even though I live in a fallen, broken world, I am also living under the strength, protection and provision of the kingdom of God. It is ever-present and available now.

What does this mean for how we live in community? How does this affect our ability to love, forgive and serve others? It means everything. We can only love, forgive, serve, bless, give, encourage, unite and have patience because we know who we are and where we live. We can do these things because Messiah Jesus has done them. We are empowered by not only his example but his life and strength. We do what he did because we are learning how to be with him in order to become like him—all through the strength he provides. The following verses are only a small portion (as you will see when you go through this book) of the many passages in the New Testament that describe how the Christ-in-us transforms the world:

Be kind to one another, tender-hearted, forgiving one another, *as God in Christ* has forgiven you. (Ephesians 4:32)

Bear with one another and, if anyone has a complaint against another, forgive each other; just *as the Lord* has forgiven you, so you also must forgive. (Colossians 3:13)

Welcome one another, therefore, just *as Christ* has welcomed you, for the glory of God. (Romans 15:7)

Husbands, love your wives, just *as Christ* loved the church and gave himself up for her. (Ephesians 5:25, italics added in all these verses)

Jesus, then, is both the model and the means of the compassion. I can live, love, serve and accept others because Jesus does those things for me. I am giving what I have, not what I lack.

This is crucial in the discussion of spiritual formation and community service. It is the way piety and action are united. Christ-in-me must be cultivated in personal exercises such as solitude, *lectio divina*, prayer, slowing down and so on. But that same Christ-in-me propels me to love others, accept them and make sacrifices of myself for them. I hope that this becomes even clearer as you read and work through this book. If not, there is a danger that our acts of service will become self-focused and ultimately self-righteous. We love, serve, forgive and care for others because God first loved, served, forgave and cared for us. The life with God we are now living is simply spilling onto everyone we meet.

Author and speaker Tony Campolo shared with me the reason for his dedication to caring for the poor. He told me that each day he sets aside time to "set his mind" on Jesus, to become aware that Christ is with him, indeed, that Christ is within him (Galatians 2:20; Colossians 1:27).

The awareness of my connection with Jesus, who lives in and through me, is what draws me to care for those in need. I see Jesus in those in need. If I did not have that foundation, my caring for them would be of no value. It would be pity, and no one wants to be pitied. I see Christ in them, and I love them. That is why I do what I do.

He offers us a brilliant description of the relationship between personal piety and social action, which shows us why we offer compassion and prevents us from doing it for the wrong reasons.

LIVING AMONG OTHERS

On an average day I wake up and greet my wife and son, help my daughter get ready for school, order food from the drive-thru at McDonald's (okay, I am not the perfect dad who cooks breakfast, and my wife leaves for work before the sun gets up, so go easy on me), encounter others in traffic, wave to other parents dropping off their kids at school, greet colleagues coming into work, teach students in the classroom, see friends at lunch, interact in meetings with colleagues and supervisors, oversee the fine work of my administrative assistant, work out next to fifty people at the gym, come home and have dinner with family or friends, help kids do homework, write, kiss my wife and family goodnight, and fall asleep. I get up and do it all over again tomorrow, with little variation.

On an average day, then, my personal kingdom will come into contact with the kingdoms and queendoms of over one hundred people, at a deeper level of engagement with some of them, at a lesser one with others. My wife and children and I know each other at the deepest relational level—called family. The lady taking my money at McDonald's does not know my name, nor I hers, but we still interact. My kingdom and her queendom (that is, what we each have say over) are briefly intertwined. The same is true with every other person on the list—colleagues, students, fellow sweaty people and fellow drivers. I may not know them well, but I live among them.

As an apprentice of Jesus the question becomes, how shall I—as a person Christ dwells in and who lives in the kingdom of God—then live among them? The family is the first place we live out our lives as apprentices of Jesus. It is also usually the most difficult place to do so. That is because of the depth of the relationship and the weight that goes with it. The family is the primary arena for us to practice kingdom living, but the second place for many people is the workplace. The average person spends 7.6 hours a day at work, which is the single largest block of our time at any one place. Naturally, we will have ample opportunity to live out our apprenticeship in the workplace.

Next in terms of time is our involvement in clubs or organizations, where we spend a lot of time interacting with others (such as the PTA, church, aerobic classes). And we cannot neglect the importance of our encounters with others in the general public—at the mall, the grocery store, the movie theater, the post office and the DMV (a very challenging place to be kind and patient!). In these places we are placed in proximity to others and thus our behavior and theirs becomes important.

COLLISION OR CONNECTION

Though these people are all different, they all have one thing in common: they are people whose kingdoms and queendoms have encountered mine. Sometimes they collide (fender-benders) and sometimes they gently connect ("My name is Rodney, and I will be your server. Can I get you something to drink, sir?"). Sometimes they tear down ("I don't want to be your friend anymore") and sometimes they build up ("I love you"). These kingdom encounters are an essential aspect of human life. They can hurt or they can help; they can curse or they can bless.

Finding success in our relationships has a lot to do with our inner condition. That is why this is the third book, and not the first, in the series. If we have grown in intimacy with the God Jesus is and reveals, our life will begin to change for the good (*The Good and Beautiful God*). If we have made strides in our struggle with lying or anger or worry, we will find that our ability to be in relationship with others will be enhanced (*The Good and Beautiful Life*). But the opposite is also true: if we are still ruled by anger, for example, learning how to love, forgive and serve others will be more challenging. I am not saying that unless you have mastered the first two books you ought not attempt this one. Sometimes we learn how to love by loving, how to forgive by forgiving and how to serve by serving. I am, however, pointing out the truth that Jesus stated: good trees bear good fruit, or the inside is what leads to the outside (Matthew 7:16-20).

Our daily encounters with others are the arenas in which our relationship with God becomes incarnate. Most of us need a little help in this area. I know I do. That is why I am writing this book—I need guidance. You are not reading the words of an expert in human relations. You are reading the journal of a novice who is sharing his struggles and insights into how we live as apprentices of Jesus in the many relationships we find ourselves. Fortunately, I have a lot of great people around me who are teaching me about this important area. This book, like the first two, is birthed in community, where the experiences of others have been an invaluable teacher.

I need to be reminded that as a follower of Jesus I am peculiar, in the best sense of that word. Peculiar, that is, to the world around me that does not live by the teachings of Jesus. My life is rooted in the eternal and strong kingdom of God; the roots of my life are in the future, safe and secure, which gives me the strength to live unselfishly, to strive for unity in the midst of diversity, to forgive even when it is not easy, to set my standards high, to live generously, to long to be worshiping in the house of the Lord and to be a witness of new life to a dying world. I need to be reminded and I need a community around me to help me remember who and whose I am, and what that means for my daily life.

This book will try to offer ways we can become blessings to the world around us. To do so, we will have to look at the reasons why we often are not, or why it is so hard to have healthy relationships with the people we meet each day. As in the first two books, a lot of failures in these areas are due to false narratives. And as in the first two books, the solution will involve correcting those false narratives by replacing them with true narratives (which are found in the Bible) as well as engaging in spiritual exercises that are aimed at embedding the right narratives into our bodies and souls.

CONFESSIONS OF AN INTROVERTED CONTEMPLATIVE

I am hopeful that this book can contribute in some way to the badly needed balance between personal spiritual formation and community engagement. As an introvert and a contemplative by nature, I have no business writing a book that deals with community and service. Though they do not come easy for me, I have labored for years, under the leading of the Spirit, to grow in these areas. My friend and coworker Matt Johnson, who is well versed in both community and service, said to me, "Jim, I think you are actually the perfect person to write this book. You are not an expert, but a fellow learner. And you know how hard it is to enter community and engage in service, whereas some of us forget about that struggle because it is easy for us. Also, you have been taking small steps through the years, and your experience will connect to more people, because most who write about social action are living too far from where most people are."

This might have been a polite way of saying, "Your lack of skill and expertise might not be a bad thing!" But I will take it as an affirmation. You will not find in these pages the words of a saint calling you to the highest level of sacrifice. (You can read books like that, and they might be what you are ready for.) Rather, you will be reading the words of a struggling straggler who is stumbling toward the light. My own failures, and occasional successes, are offered as an encouragement as we labor to love our neighbor. Our ultimate teacher is the Holy Spirit, who I trust will lead us into all truth, correct us when we steer off course, and infuse us with energy and encouragement as we run the race set before us (Hebrews 12:1-2). May the blessings of God the Father, Son and Holy Spirit be upon you as you labor to live the good and beautiful life in your good and beautiful communities.

HOW to get the most out of this book

This book is intended to be used in the context of a community—a small group, a Sunday school class, or a few friends gathered in a home or coffee shop. Working through this book with others greatly magnifies the impact. If you go through this on your own, only the first four suggestions below will apply to you. No matter how you use it, I am confident that God can and will accomplish a good work in you.

1. Prepare. Find a journal or notebook with blank pages.
You will use this journal to answer the questions sprinkled throughout each chapter and for the reflections on the soul-training experience found at the end of each chapter.

2. Read. Read each chapter thoroughly.
Try not to read hurriedly, and avoid reading the chapter at the last minute. Start reading early enough in the week so that you have time to digest the material.

3. Do. Complete the weekly exercise(s).
Engaging in exercises related to the content of the chapter you have just read will help deepen the ideas you are learning and will begin to mold and heal your soul. Some of the exercises will take more time to complete than others. Be sure to leave plenty of time to do the exercise before your group meeting. You want to have time not only to do the exercise but also to do the written reflections.

4. Reflect. Make time to complete your written reflections.
In your journal go through the questions posed throughout and at the end of each chapter. This will help you clarify your thoughts and crystallize what God is teaching you. It will also help with the next part.

5. Interact. Come to the group time prepared to listen and to share.
Here is where you get a chance to hear and learn from others' experiences and insights. If everyone takes time to journal in advance, the conversation in the group time will be much more effective. People will be sharing from their more distilled thoughts, and the group time will be more valuable. It is important to remember that we should listen twice as much as we speak! But do be prepared to share. The other group members will learn from your ideas and experiences.

6. Encourage. Interact with each other—outside of group time.
One of the great blessings technology brings is the ease with which we can stay in touch. It is a good idea to send an encouraging email to at least two others in your group between meeting times. Let them know you are thinking of them, and ask how you can pray for them. This will strengthen relationships and deepen your overall experience. Building strong relationships is a key factor in making your experience a success.

one

The peculiar community

When I was growing up, my family attended a very serious, cold and orderly Methodist church. The preacher had been there for twenty-five years, and over time the church reflected his personality. He was a scholar with strong speaking skills and dry humor. He particularly loved elegance and order. For years I wondered why there was a telephone—an olive green telephone—right next to the massive wooden chair the pastor sat in during the service. One day a child became whiny and started to cry during one of the quiet, reflective moments of prayer, and I opened my eyes and saw the pastor pick up the phone. Within seconds an usher came up to the pew where the child was misbehaving and escorted the mother and the child out of the sanctuary.

I got the message: children must be seen but not heard. This made a big impression on me as a child. The narrative was embedded in my little brain that church was a solemn place. No one spoke to one another during the service. I remember getting "shushed" a lot. Only afterward, during coffee time, did people interact. My parents came for the service to sing the hymns, enjoy the choir's anthem and listen to a good sermon. But as a child none of that mattered to me. I didn't like the hymns. I could not understand the Bible, much less the sermon. The pews were uncomfortable, and everyone had to be quiet and still, which is not natural to children (possible, but not enjoyable). The only part I liked was when we had Communion (four times a year), because I got a snack—albeit a small one consisting of a cube of bread and a tiny cup of grape juice.

We went less and less as I got older (and I was thankful), and eventually I stopped going altogether, except on Christmas and Easter. Mom insisted. I had no idea I was developing a theology, an understanding of God and communal life, but I was. Those early experiences shaped how I thought about God. God hovered above his neat and orderly, somber and sad followers. I could not wait to get home, take off my clip-on tie and run to the field to play baseball with my friends. The next Sunday I would pray (ironically) that something would come up and we would not have to go to church. Spending time with God's assembled people was, in my young mind, a dreadful thing. Though I might have been too young to notice, there did not seem to be anything special about this gathering of people. Church people were just regular people doing their religious duty of one hour a week.

> How have your early experiences with church or with Christians shaped your view of community?

Then, when I turned eighteen, things began to change. My soul was restless and I was on a search for meaning that eventually led me to give Jesus a chance. He reciprocated and started changing my life. Within a few months I was reading the Bible daily, praying a lot and hanging out with two other Christian guys. When I went to college, I knew that it would be hard to continue my faith on my own, so I prayed for some support, and it came in the first week I was on campus. A guy I played sports against in high school noticed my "fish" necklace, asked if I was a Christian and invited me to come to a Bible fellowship.

It was a Wednesday evening I will never forget. I walked into a room in one of the dorms and was confronted by several alien things. First, the room was packed with students. In my church the youth group was very small. Second, they all seemed excited to be there. I had never seen anyone excited about church. (Could you call this a church?) Third, it was a gathering of dissimilar people. There were some jocks and academic types; there were males and females, blacks and whites; there were some very pretty girls and some handsome guys, and some not so pretty or handsome. The church I grew up in comprised all-white, middle-class people between forty and sixty years old. Finally, the thing that stood out about the makeup of this gathering was the number of handicapped people, most of them in wheelchairs, but some of them with mental challenges.

What is going on? I thought to myself.

A few minutes later the leader stood up and welcomed everyone, and the room felt very warm and inviting. I felt what I could only describe as *goodness* in the air. Then a young man and a young woman led us in a time of praise and worship music, with only a guitar and their voices. It was something I had never seen: fifty people jammed into a room singing loudly and joyfully, some with hands lifted in the air, as if they were in a moment of ecstasy. Some jumped up and down, some clapped, and everyone in the room (except me at that point) seemed entranced—in a good way. After twenty minutes of praise-singing the leader, a senior, taught from the Bible. He was very transparent as he spoke about his own life and struggles, and he was also very gifted as a teacher. He made the Bible make sense to me and helped connect it to my life, to things that mattered to me, things I was struggling to understand.

Afterward I thanked the young man who had invited me. He asked if I would come back, which I affirmed without hesitation. I did not know why at the time, but I later would discover that I had just witnessed something my soul was designed to experience: a good and beautiful community. They were not perfect (the singing was not professional, but good enough), nor did I suddenly want to become best friends with everyone in the room (the guy next to me really needed to take a shower). Perfection, elegance, talent and performance did not draw me, but the fellowship, the togetherness, the unity in diversity intrigued me. These people were very peculiar. And I liked it.

FALSE NARRATIVE: CHRISTIANS ARE NO DIFFERENT

As in most of the false narratives we have looked at, this one is partially true. According to most of the surveys and polls I have seen, Christians behave in much the same way non-Christians do, at least in the United States. The divorce rate of Christians and non-Christians is about the same, for example. The percentage of teenagers engaged in premarital sex is about the only poll I have seen where there was much of a difference between believers and nonbelievers, but even then there was only a 5 percent difference. So, yes, in some ways the behavior of those who claim to be following Christ is not much different than those who do not. And when you add in a few high-profile failures among Christian leaders, it begins to seem like Christians are not only not any better, but they might be worse.

I want to examine that for a moment. If a CEO or an accountant is caught in an adulterous affair, it is not likely to make the news at all. But when a pastor is caught in an affair or embezzling money, it is a big deal. Which leads us to question why. Why is it newsworthy if a religious figure has a moral failure? Because they ought not do that. In other words, we *expect* them to be different. Why? Because they *claim* to be different, and for the most part they intend to be different.

And quite often they are different. In the city where I live, there are three hospitals. All were started and are still owned by Christian groups. Regardless of your faith background, if you need a kidney transplant it will be done by the people at St. Francis, St. Joseph or

Wesley Hospital. There are many soup kitchens, homeless shelters, rescue missions and homes for battered women. Nearly all of them are run by Christians. Throughout the ages, Christians have led the way in the care and support of people in need.

The true narrative is this: Christians are not always different, but they ought to be, and often are. In this chapter you will meet some of the Christians—individuals as well as groups—who are truly different. In chapter two we will examine where the difference comes from and how we can change our minds and hearts to become people who stand out from the rest of the world—in a good way. You might even call us peculiar.

TRUE NARRATIVE: CHRISTIANS ARE PECULIAR

I first came across the idea of the peculiarity of God's gathered people from a passage in the King James Bible: "But ye are a chosen generation, a royal priesthood, an holy nation, *a peculiar people;* that ye should shew forth the praises of him who hath called you out of darkness into his marvellous light" (1 Peter 2:9, italics added).

I love the word *peculiar.* Dictionaries define it as "distinctive," "odd," "strange" and "weird." In a word, peculiar means *different.* Different from the ordinary, the common, from everyone else. Christians are peculiar in that they are different from everyone else.

But are apprentices of Jesus really so different? I believe we are, or at least we ought to be. For example, if I (by the power of the Spirit) begin telling the

> What do you think of when you hear the word *peculiar?*

truth in my life, I will become an oddity. If I can learn to slow down, live without being ruled by anger and actually pray for people who try to cut me down, I will be considered weird, because this world does not work this way. Only people who are steeped in the kingdom of God can begin living this way. There are far too few.

To be sure, there are non-apprentices who tell the truth, live without anger and can be nice to people who are not nice to them. Christ-followers do not have exclusive rights to the virtues. The difference is in how and why we live this way. We do so because we are following the example of Jesus, our teacher, and are being led by the Holy Spirit, our strength and comforter. And we are living in the strong and sustaining kingdom of God. We have from the very beginning.

HOW CHRISTIANS ARE DIFFERENT

In an early Christian document known as the *Epistle to Diognetus* (c. A.D. 120-200), the author wrote a response to some propaganda circulating in the Roman Empire. People had spread false rumors about the Christians, saying that they were a dangerous, secret society filled with bizarre behavior. People were saying slanderous things about Christians, such as they practiced cannibalism (because during Communion they ate the "body and the blood of Jesus"). The epistle is believed to have been written by a man named Athenagoras. In one important section the author describes how Christians are alike—and different—from others.

> The difference between Christians and the rest of mankind is not a matter of nationality, or language, or customs. Christians do not live in separate cities of their own, speak any special dialect, nor practice any eccentric way of life. . . . They pass their lives in whatever township—Greek or foreign—each man's lot has determined; and conform to ordinary local usage in their clothing, diet, and other habits. Nevertheless, the organization of their community does exhibit some features that are remarkable, and even surprising. For instance, though they are residents at home in their own countries, their behavior there is more like transients. . . . Though destiny has placed them here in the flesh, they do not live after the flesh; their days are passed on earth, but their citizenship is above in the heavens. They obey the pre-

scribed laws, but in their own private lives they transcend the laws. They show love to all men—and all men persecute them. They are misunderstood, and condemned; yet by suffering death they are quickened into life. They are poor, yet making many rich; lacking all things, yet having all things in abundance. . . . They repay [curses] with blessings, and abuse with courtesy. For the good they do, they suffer stripes as evildoers.

I find this quote fascinating. Athenagoras spells out the ways Christians were the same as all people, as well as the ways they were peculiar. In outward ways they were no different from anyone else in the Roman Empire. They lived in the same homes, wore the same clothes and ate the same food as the average Roman citizen. They obeyed the laws—no one accused them of be-

> Does the church today sound like the church Athenagoras describes? Why or why not?

ing thieves, of not paying their taxes or of harming others. Athenagoras is saying, "We are just like you."

And yet they were different. They obeyed earthly laws but lived by higher laws ("You have heard that it was said, . . . 'You shall not murder.' . . . But I say to you . . ." [Matthew 5:21-22]). They were members of the Roman Empire, but this world was not their home; their citizenship was in heaven (Colossians 3:1-2; Philippians 3:20). They endured suffering well and even blessed those who cursed them, as their teacher taught them to do—and as he himself did. I think my favorite part of the quote is where Athenagoras writes, "For the good they do . . ." This is an easily overlooked point: *the good they do*. It is no small thing to do good. Especially in a world in which there is so much wrongdoing. I suppose you could say that it was the good they did that got them into such trouble. It was, and is, peculiar to do good things for no good reason. People get suspicious.

Despite the false accusations and the persecutions, Christianity not only survived, it actually flourished. According to secular historian Rodney Stark, Christianity grew exponentially from its inception, at the astonishing growth rate of 40 percent per decade. Figure 1.1 gives a clear illustration of the rapid growth:

Year	Number of Christians	Percent of the Population
A.D. 40	1,000	0.0017
A.D. 100	7,530	0.0126
A.D. 200	217,195	0.36
A.D. 250	1,171,356	1.9
A.D. 300	6,299,832	10.5
A.D. 350	33,882,008	56.5

Figure 1.1. Christians as a percentage of the world's population

What can account for such a growth rate, especially given the danger involved in being a Christ-follower? I have heard many explanations, but the one that I find most appealing is that the lives Christians were living were so winsome that others simply wanted to have what they had.

The same is true today. Several years ago I recruited a young woman to play tennis for our team at Friends University. Her father said to me on the phone, "Is your college one of those places that beats people over the head with the Bible? Because we have not raised her to be religious, and we are concerned about that." I told him that we never beat people with anything—being Quaker and all. But I did tell him that there were some wonderful Christian people she would be exposed to. He was fine with that. He just wanted her to have freedom of choice, and I assured him she did.

A few months after being at the school, she noticed the vibrant lives of many of the students on our campus who were followers of Jesus but never pushed anything on her. I never once engaged in a conversation with her about God or Jesus or the Bible, but she did come to our campus fellowship. She went home over Christmas break, and when she returned she said, "I wanted to tell you that I gave my life to Jesus during the break." After much rejoicing I asked her, "What made you want to do that?" She said, "After seeing all of these people who have peace and joy and love, I wanted to have what they have."

After two thousand years not much changes.

A PECULIAR GOD

Why are Christians peculiar (or at least ought to be)? It is because our God is peculiar. The God we love and serve is extraordinarily different than the gods humans design. When the Greeks and Romans created their pantheon of gods and goddesses, they looked remarkably like humans—often at their worst. Their gods lied and cheated and murdered. They committed adultery and punished each other out of anger and jealousy. The stories of the gods are fascinating to read. There's lots of intrigue.

The God that Jesus reveals is peculiar. This God loves humans so much that he became one of them and died for them. This God forgives when it is not deserved. This God is generous, never vengeful. If the God of Jesus displays wrath, it is only because this God is good and loving, and is rightly against sin because it hurts his beloved children. No one could have made this story up. There is nothing like it in all of religious literature. That is because in all of the other religions there is no God like the one Jesus revealed.

God's ways are not our ways, and God's thoughts are not our thoughts (Isaiah 55:8). God's values are different. He is like a father who gets mistreated by a wayward son and aches for him to come home (Luke 15:11-32). That was a peculiar notion to Jesus' hearers. God is like an employer who gives a day's pay to workers who worked only an hour (Matthew 20:1-16). Jesus shocked people with that narrative. "What kind of God is this?" the people must have murmured. Jesus revealed a God who was like no other god the world had ever heard of. This God was indeed peculiar.

So it is not surprising that God's people would also be peculiar. One of my favorite passages in the Bible is in 1 John. It reveals the origin of Christian oddity:

> Beloved, let us love one another, because love is from God; everyone who loves is born of God and knows God. Whoever does not love does not know God, for God is love. God's love was revealed among us in this way: God sent his only Son into the world so that we might live through him. In this is love, not that we loved God but that he loved us and sent his Son to be the atoning sacrifice for our sins. Beloved, since God loved us so much, we also ought to love one another. No one has ever seen God; if we love one another, God lives in us, and his love is perfected in us. (1 John 4:7-12)

The ethic is simple: as God is, so should his people be. If we do not love, we must not know God. Because "God's love was revealed among us" in the person of Jesus "that we might live through him."

We do what we do because Jesus is living in and through us (Galatians 2:20). And notice how John stresses that God loved us before we loved God, that God loved a people who did not love or serve him. That, John said, is the kind of love we ought to give to one another. And the end of the passage drives home the point one last time: when we love, God lives in us, and his love completes us. So our peculiar God transforms us into peculiar people, people who love others, even if they do not love us in return.

And so our history is strewn with odd people. The martyrs sang hymns while being executed. Unheard of. Francis of Assisi left his wealthy home and walked naked out of town, put on a beggar's cloak, and kissed lepers. Strange, indeed. Catherine of Genoa (1447-1510) and her rich husband left a lifestyle that made them feel empty, moved into a modest home, and decided to devote themselves to the care of the sick and suffering. She spent several hours a day in prayer, during which she said she felt the burning flame of God's presence in her heart, and she spent twice as many hours caring for those in need, living a brilliant rhythm of contemplation and action. Weird.

In more contemporary days William Graham left his Bible college and served a small church in Chicago, forgoing seminary because he wanted to preach so badly. He later joined the staff of Youth for Christ to minister to young people. He later started preaching about morality and peace and justice, but mainly he led people to Christ—hundreds of thousands of people. Most people know him as "Billy," but to the world he is a strange phenomenon.

My sister's church held the funeral of a young man who had been living an openly homosexual lifestyle, and for doing so they were picketed by members of another church who held signs that said "God Hates Fags." It was a chilly, rainy morning. The people at my sister's church were shocked at the rage and anger of these people who claimed to be followers of Jesus. Though they were being cursed, they decided to bless the picketers. They brought out trays full of hot cocoa and offered it to them. How odd.

The Quakers who lived in the United States in the eighteenth century came to abhor the injustice of slavery. They held a meeting in New Jersey, under the leadership of the Holy Spirit and a man named John Woolman. They prayed for hours in silence. Then, they decided to free all of their slaves. That is not all. They also decided that they should pay back these former slaves all of the money owed them for their labors. It was a radical idea that some suspected would bankrupt all of them. Amazingly it didn't. Still, the whole thing ran so counter to the rest of culture, almost no one could believe it. Crazy.

Shane Claiborne lives—intentionally—among the poor in inner-city Philadelphia and spends time trying to help people improve their lives. Mostly he just loves people, the kind of people the rest of the world would just as soon ignore. The young

Who do you see as "peculiar" examples in your life or in church history?

woman I mentioned earlier who gave her life to Christ after being moved by the lives of others on her campus is now living in intentional community in a poor neighborhood with her husband and two other couples; they use their time and resources to help draw people together. Those who live in their neighborhood think they are really strange, and love them for it. Their block parties give hope and joy to people who find such feelings hard to come by.

Ain't that peculiar?

You might even call these people maladjusted. And if you did it would be a compliment. Because they are *maladjusted* to the ways of this world. Of course, not every Christian is maladjusted in this way, but I think we ought to be. Professor Cornel West put it well when he said, "There have always been Christians who are well-adjusted to greed, well-adjusted to fear, well-adjusted to bigotry. There have always been Christians who are maladjusted to greed, maladjusted to fear, and maladjusted to bigotry."

Not all Christian are, but all Christians *ought* to be maladjusted to things like injustice, greed, materialism and racism. Too often we easily become well-adjusted to these things. I know I have. It is easy to become well-adjusted to the culture we live in, the one that uses hate and violence to gain control, the one that treats people as objects for personal gain, the one that winks at immorality.

Reflect on the idea that, as A. W. Tozer has said, we are "too much at home in the world." What are your thoughts about that?

Dr. West says elsewhere: "It takes courage to ask—how did I become so well-adjusted to injustice? It takes courage to cut against the grain and become non-conformist. It takes courage to wake up and stay awake instead of engaging in complacent slumber. It takes courage to shatter conformity and cowardice." I agree. It takes courage to live like our peculiar God, to love and forgive the unlovely and the unforgivable. The only way we will ever find this courage is when we discover that we are a community of people who are rooted in another world. That is the subject of chapter two.

TRUST THE LEADING OF THE SPIRIT

One of my favorite stories illustrates an important principle whose application will come back to us over and over again—especially in this book. It involves two of the leading figures in Quaker history: George Fox and William Penn. George Fox (1624-1691) was the founder of the Quakers, a Christian movement, in seventeenth-century England. Two of the great Quaker contributions are their teaching on pacifism (refusal to use violence) and equality (abolishing class distinction).

William Penn (1644-1718) grew up in the upper class and had the best education available. At the age of twenty-three, Penn became a Quaker, and soon after everything began to change. It was common in Penn's day to wear a sword, which was not intended to harm anyone but was a sign that the wearer belonged to the upper class. After becoming a Quaker, Penn struggled with whether he should wear the sword. After all, it was a symbol of war as well as class distinction—two things Quakers stood squarely against.

So Penn went to Fox, his mentor, to seek guidance on the matter. "May I continue to wear the sword?" he asked Fox. I would have expected Fox to say, "No, you must get rid of it. Turn it into a plowshare and never wear anything like it again." Instead, George Fox offered a response that is a touchstone for me in the area of Christian living. He said, "Wear it as long as you can, William, wear it as long as you can."

Fox was laying out an important principle in the Christian life. When it comes to our practices and behavior, *we need to avoid making rules and laws, and trust the leading of the Spirit.* Fox did not say, "Don't wear it," nor did he say, "It's all right to wear it." He trusted that Penn would make the right decision in time. Had Fox given him a command, he would have robbed Penn of the opportunity to listen to the Holy Spirit, and he would have put in place a rigid standard, which almost always leads to later problems.

NEITHER LEGALISM NOR LICENSE

In a book about how we ought to live, there is always a danger of laying down rules. In this book we will examine the lifestyle choices and practices that some men and women make, which you may find impressive or encouraging. We will look at people and churches whose generosity is impressive, whose forgiveness is amazing and whose witness to nonbelievers is inspiring. Their examples are meant to encourage us, but we must be careful not to make their practices the only way, the right way or even the best way to live as an apprentice of Jesus. For example, I mentioned my friends Matt and Catherine, who live with two other couples in a large house. Their frugality and love for their neighborhood is very impressive. But if I were to conclude from their example that true Christians must live communally, I would be misguided. There is a tendency to turn individual, Spirit-led practices into corporate laws.

So I will apply the "Fox principle" a lot in this book. When we raise the issues of how we use our wealth, how we spend our time or what practices might enhance our life with God, and which practices might impede that relationship, we need to remember the wisdom of George Fox. For example, during the course of this book some of you who have financial means may be led to ask, *Is it okay for me to drive this car and live in this house?* The last thing you should do is answer with a hard-and-fast rule (for example, "no Christian should own a home over $100,000, or drive a car worth more than $20,000"). Instead, we should say, "Live in it and drive it as long as you feel comfortable, as long as you feel no unease in your spirit."

Some may see this as a cop-out. To be sure, there are some laws that cannot be broken without harm in our lives (such as the Ten Commandments). I would never say to a man who is having an affair, "Continue the affair as long as you feel comfortable." But when it comes to the many lifestyle questions we face, in terms of what we eat or drink or wear or drive, we need to think sensibly and with an ear to the whisper of the Spirit. The kingdom of God is not about rules, but about the goodness and confidence and laughter we discover when we let the Holy Spirit lead us.

I intend to take the same position as George Fox and the apostle Paul. I will encourage you to come to your own conclusions on these matters, under the leading of the Spirit, and to avoid turning them into laws that all others must obey, or judging those who do not do as you do. Should Christians wear jewelry? Or watch television? Or go to the movies? Or play sports on Sundays? There are good Christian men and women who would answer no to each of these questions, and good Christians who answer yes to them. Just because there is no right or wrong answer for all does not mean they are not worth asking. In fact, I think the process of asking the questions and listening to the Spirit in our individual lives is both necessary and inspiring. We want black and white answers, but often that is just because we are lazy and unwilling to do the challenging work of discernment.

You might have guessed that William Penn gave up wearing the sword, but not right away. That too is instructive. As our narratives and practices change, so do other things in our lives, but not overnight. I would like to think that the young Penn learned a valuable lesson from Fox, one that he would apply many times throughout his life. And it was an amazing life. Penn later came to America and establised Quaker communities, eventually leading the fight against slavery. William Penn was an amazing person in many respects—as a Christian (his book *No Cross, No Crown* is inspiring) and as a statesman.

An example of how we avoid legalism and license is through the practice of soul-training experiences. These exercises are not laws that bind us, nor are they practices we can neglect if we want to grow in our life with God and with one another. They stretch us and awaken us to the leading of the Spirit without becoming a recipe with a predictable outcome.

two-by-four

There are two essential points in this chapter. The first is that Christians are peculiar. The second is that their peculiarity comes from following their peculiar God. Put another way, as we spend time with this peculiar God, we will become more and more peculiar ourselves. But this will not happen without our cooperation. For this reason I am asking you to do two things this week: (1) spend time with God and (2) do some peculiar things. Remember, *peculiar* is not bad, just something different from what our culture is used to seeing.

This week I would like you to wed contemplation with action, personal piety with social justice. We need to keep a balance between spending time with God and caring for others. To lose one or the other is a common, but deadly, mistake. As a way of staying balanced, I would like you to do two things: spend two hours focused on God and do four intentional acts of peculiarity. I call it "two-by-four": two hours with God and four acts of kindness. I will offer some guidance about how to spend the two hours, and I will suggest some things you might want to do in terms of helping others.

TWO HOURS WITH GOD

Some of you are probably intimidated by spending two hours with God, and others are thinking, *That's it—only two hours?* After a lot of interaction with people and careful reflection, I think this is a very attainable amount of time. It is neither too much nor too little. Of course, the two hours is a suggestion, not a law. It is something to aim for, but not something to make you feel either proud because you did it or guilty because you did not. Let me explain why I think it is attainable, and offer some guidance about how to spend that time with God.

HOW WILL I MANAGE TWO HOURS?

First, the two hours do not have to be done all at once. I would recommend thirty minutes on four separate occasions. (Some may spend eight times of fifteen minutes. Others may want to spend two one-hour sessions with God.)

Second, corporate worship (going to church) can also count for one of your hours, but only if you go to church with a sense that you are meeting God, that your focus is on God. Too often we spend much of our time in church services thinking about things other than God. Here are some tips for how to go to church well:

- Arrive early.

- Take time to focus on God before the service begins.

- Remind yourself over and over that God is the focus.

- When you get distracted, turn back to thinking about God.

So, you may want to go to church and then schedule one or more blocks of time when you will give your attention to God.

SUGGESTED WAYS TO SPEND TIME WITH GOD

The final exercise in the second book in this series, *The Good and Beautiful Life*, is about how to spend a day devotionally, with guidance from Madame Guyon. Keying off of her ideas, I offer the following suggestions for other ways to spend time with God. The following steps are offered not as rigid rules but as suggestions.

1. Find a quiet, restful place to be alone. It should be a place where you feel comfortable and are relatively free from interruptions.

2. Breathe. It takes time to become "present where we are." One of the things I like to do is simply breathe and pay attention to my breathing. It calms me and helps me focus. Sometimes I actually count my breaths and have found that somewhere around forty I am in a relaxed but concentrated state.

3. *Say a prayer.* I like to pray the Lord's Prayer or the doxology. The main thing is to remember that you are in the presence of God.

4. *Praise.* I like the phrase *God inhabits the praises of his people.* Take a little time to write out a list of your blessings (you may have completed an exercise like this in *The Good and Beautiful God*). Then thank God for them. Expect to feel a lift in your spirit.

5. *Read reflectively.* You might want to open your Bible and read a short passage. I suggest no more than four or five verses. The Psalms or the Gospels are good places to start. Others find a daily devotional helpful. I like reading a short passage from *The Imitation of Christ.*

6. *Ponder.* Spend some time thinking about what you have just read. Is there a message for you in it? What might God be saying to you in that passage or selection?

7. *Ask and listen.* Don't be afraid to speak to God directly. Ask God any questions you have. But don't expect an audible answer. Learning to discern the still, small voice of God is an acquired ability that takes time and practice. Sometimes God speaks in a quiet inner voice, and sometimes God speaks to me through a series of thoughts that come to mind.

The key is to allow your heart to be exposed to God. Let God know how you are feeling. The Psalms are wonderful for this very reason; the psalmist is not afraid to let the anger or anguish, praise or thanksgiving be made known to God.

8. *Journal.* It is helpful to write down your thoughts and feelings during these quiet times with God. Jot down your thoughts or questions in a journal. It helps crystallize what you are learning and offers a written record you will find valuable in the years to come.

I hope this offers you some basic ideas about how to use your time. These eight steps can be done in twenty to thirty minutes or, at a leisurely pace, can take up forty-five minutes to an hour.

FOUR ACTS OF PECULIARITY

Several years ago I participated in an exercise in which I was to try to do one *unselfish and unexpected act of kindness or generosity* each day, for thirty straight days. I really enjoyed the exercise. It forced me to think more about what I could do for other people, and it gave me the encouragement to actually carry them out. I found myself doing a lot of little things for people (taking someone's tray back in the cafeteria) and occasionally larger things (helping friends move). It also forced me to be creative because, believe it or not, doing one unexpected and unselfish act of kindness *every day* is harder than you might think. Fortunately, the person who created the exercise told us ahead of time that it would be hard, so at least we were not surprised.

The only thing I did not like about it was precisely that problem. I found myself forcing my acts of kindness in places where it was not welcome or needed. And I found myself faking a bit. (Is waving at a stranger an unexpected act of kindness?) After a few years I decided to find a more attainable yet still transforming approach. Instead of one-a-day, I challenged myself to do four unselfish and unexpected acts of kindness or generosity *each week*. This really helped me, because sometimes there is nothing to do, but on other days three for four opportunities may arise.

The next thing I discovered was that I could also expand the exercise to include doing things that indicate I am maladjusted to this world. For example, if I choose not to buy something I do not need, I am showing I am maladjusted to the greed, materialism and excess of this world. If I resist the temptation to treat people according to their social class (usually indicated by dress) and treat all people as equal to me and to one another, I am showing that this world is not my home; I belong to the kingdom of God. If I decide to slow down and avoid rushing, I am demonstrating that I am maladjusted to the culture of hurry I live in.

By opening my experiment up to include these kinds of things, it really got interesting. I was intentionally doing things that I might otherwise not have done, and doing them with a sense that I am a citizen of another world. Kindness and generosity, to be sure, are peculiar activities of the highest kind. So I would like you to concentrate, especially this week, on planning *four unselfish acts of kindness, acts of peculiarity or acts of maladjustment.*

Here are some examples of the things I have enjoyed doing:

1. Ask for someone's car keys and take the car to a car wash, or wash it by hand.

2. Rake the leaves or sweep the driveway of your neighbor.

3. Be intentional in conversation, inviting people to talk about their lives. (Listening is a great gift.)

4. Clean up the house or apartment without being asked (assuming you share space with others; if not, you are doing a kind act to yourself!).

5. Pay for the person behind you in the drive-thru.

6. Intentionally go to a place of business in a part of town that is struggling economically.

7. Let others go ahead of you in line.

8. Engage with people by saying, "Hi, how are you today?" and then wait for an answer—don't just walk on.

two

The Hopeful Community

My wife is a very social person. She loves being with groups of people, having dinners, celebrating special occasions or just hanging out with her friends. She is an elementary school teacher, which means she spends a lot of time socializing and meeting new people as part of her job. When someone learns that she is the wife of a religion professor who is also a minister, they often ask her questions about God and faith. Once in a while the discussion turns to serious questions such as, How could a good God allow evil? or Why are there so many religions, and how do you know yours is right? Sometimes people are genuinely seeking answers and perhaps even seeking God. She comes home from these discussions and invariably says the same thing: "I wish you had been there."

She says this because she thinks that I would be able to answer their questions. Every time she says this I respond, "It would not have made a difference if I had been there. Most of the questions they are asking are not the real issue. They are usually smoke screens hiding something else. What they really want to know is, 'Is it true?' and the answer to that is not in an intellectual idea but in a changed life.

That is something you can give them. Your life is your witness. You have something real, something you know to be true in your depths, and it has shaped who you are. You do not have to do anything to witness to that life, and you could not hide it if you tried. *They want to know the reason you have hope.*" Still, she says she wishes she could better articulate her faith when she is asked. She concludes, "I guess evangelism is not my gift." Actually, it is one of her gifts.

While it is true that some people are more naturally gifted at witnessing, evangelism or faith sharing, all apprentices of Jesus can and do share their faith with others, whether they are conscious of it or not. There are two ways to share our faith: with our life and with our mouth. Our life is the most profound witness to our connection with God. Most of the time we are witnessing to others by our actions. But there are also times when people give us permission to explain what we believe and why we believe it. In this chapter I want to address the two ways we share our faith by looking first at how we can better speak with our lives and second, at how we can learn to "give an answer to everyone who asks [us] to give the reason for [our] hope" (1 Peter 3:15 NIV).

> How does one of your spiritual gifts enable you to share the reason you have hope?

FALSE NARRATIVE: ONLY CERTAIN PEOPLE CAN SHARE THEIR FAITH

It is true, there are people who are particularly gifted in the area of witnessing to nonbelievers. They typically have an unwavering confidence, an undaunted courage, to speak the truth to people who may reject them. They also are typically gifted with words. But the narrative that only some people have the gift of evangelism can become an excuse for those without the gift to refrain from evangelism. To be honest, sharing our faith can be intimidating. The following is a list of statements I have heard Christians make through the years:

- I am not good at it. I have tried, and I just stammered and stuttered.

- I have seen people witnessing, and I would be embarrassed to try.

- I am afraid I will offend if I share my faith.

- I would feel like a hypocrite if I shared my faith—I am not a perfect Christian.

- If I bring up my faith, I am afraid they will reject me.

- I cannot share my faith with others because I am not educated enough.

These are real concerns. Sharing our faith can be embarrassing, and at times it comes across as offensive. None of us are perfect, so we all could be accused of hypocrisy. And there is always the possibility of rejection.

Still, none of these objections are completely true. Even if we are not good at evangelism, we can get better. Though it can be embarrassing, it does not have to be. There is the possibility of offending someone, but not if we do it well. We are not perfect, but our

> Think of a person whose life was a witness to you. What was it that you found winsome about his or her life?

own perfection is not our claim; we are pointing not to ourselves but to One who is perfect. We run the risk of rejection, but the sacred worth of the person we are sharing with, and the potential life-changing gain, makes it a risk worth taking. Though it may seem intimidating, in truth, we are already sharing our faith every day, and it is something that we can improve on. The secret lies not in learning new techniques or special arts of persuasion or in becoming so perfect in our life that others marvel and ask, "How can I be like you?" The answer, ultimately, is found in our story. The story shapes our actions, and when we know it well, we can tell it well with words.

TRUE NARRATIVE: ALL CHRISTIANS
SHARE THEIR FAITH

When I was a fairly new Christian, I remember hearing the cliché "You are the only Bible some people will read." I thought it was profound, but I have to admit that I also found it intimidating. I didn't feel up to that assignment. "Jim, you are the only hope for so-and-so. They won't read the Bible; they don't even have one. So we are counting on you." The implication was that my life was the only witness to Jesus this person would have, and I knew that my life did not measure up. Still, the cliché is true. There are a vast number of people who are not following Jesus, and we see them each day; they have not opened a Bible recently, if ever, so their only connection to the faith is us. It is challenging, but it need not be intimidating. There is a solution.

In every aspect of our lives, we know that there are ways to improve, to get better at something, from learning a language to playing an instrument to doing a job. Over the last several years my wife, Meghan, has done a lot of things to improve her ability to teach. Through classes, books, seminars and trying new techniques, she has become a better teacher. My son, Jacob, plays baseball. He trains his body through exercise and practice; with that and some excellent coaching, he has improved each year as a pitcher. One coach taught him a new grip, which made a vast improvement. My daughter Hope is a pretty talented artist for her age, but it was only when we enrolled her in an after-school art program that we began to see what she was capable of. With excellent instruction and guidance, her technique improved quickly. After the course, her drawings were markedly better.

These stories illustrate a fundamental fact of our lives: there are ways to improve what we do. But when it comes to our faith life, we seem to think it is "a mystery wrapped in an enigma." I hear people say, "I am not a good pray-er, like so and so," as if prayer were a sacred skill given to certain people. Prayer is an activity we can get better at. The same is true with sharing our faith. We are already doing it, though not always well. So we might as well find ways to improve. But before we examine the two ways we share our faith—words and actions—I want to turn our attention to their foundation: *the story.* The more you understand that story, the more it becomes your story; the more it becomes your story, the more naturally it will come forth in your words and actions.

THE STORY THAT INSPIRES HOPE

Sometimes when we read the Bible we gloss over some of the words, especially the ones we hear a lot, like *faith, love* and *hope.* This happened to me while memorizing Colossians 1:5: "the faith and love that spring from the hope that is stored up for you in heaven." In order for me to fully understand the verse, it had to be connected to the verses that precede and follow it. Paul writes:

> We always thank God, the Father of our Lord Jesus Christ, when we pray for you, because we have heard of your faith in Christ Jesus and of the love you have for all the saints—the faith and love that *spring from the hope* that is stored up for you in heaven and that you have already heard about in the word of truth, the gospel that has come to you. (Colossians 1:3-6 NIV, italics added)

Here is the main point: *faith and love come from hope.* Hope is seldom thought of as the origin of faith and love, but that is what Paul is saying here. Bible scholar N. T. Wright puts it this way: "The solid facts about the future hope of Christians are a powerful motivation for constant faith and costly love in the present." Note his words *solid facts.* That is the key.

By definition, hope is "confidence in a good future." Faith does not live in a vacuum; it must attach itself to something. We must believe *in* something. That is why Paul says, "we have heard of your faith *in* Christ Jesus . . . because of the hope . . ." Our hope is rooted in heaven (v. 5), where Christ is seated at the right hand of God.

Every time Paul wrote "you" or "your" in the Colossians passage, he used the second person plural: "the hope that is stored up for you" is the hope we share as a community. Hope is not just mine. Apprentices of Jesus share in that same hope. It binds us together and increases our love for one another. It is not just the hope of an individual but of a community.

The Christian community "has its roots in the future and its branches in the present," writes John D. Zizioulas. The *ecclesia* (church, community) of Jesus finds its origins in the future. And that future is bright, certain and unshakable because of Jesus and his finished work. Hope is the bridge from the future into the present, and the branches of that hope are faith and love.

N. T. Wright says that "a mission-shaped church must have its mission shaped by hope; that the genuine Christian hope, rooted in Jesus' resurrection, is the hope for God's renewal of all things, for his overcoming of corruption, decay, and death, for his filling of the whole cosmos with his love and grace, his power and glory." Roots in the future, roots in the resurrection, roots in the eternal victory of Jesus, roots that are firmly planted in eternal life, roots that nourish the trunk and the branches, and ultimately produce the fruit that draws others into the story. Wright concludes, "To be truly effective in this kind of mission, one must be genuinely and cheerfully rooted in God's renewal." We have a real reason to cheer. The more we know the story, the more we rejoice.

What do you hope for?

THE FOUR-PART STORY OF HOPE

Paul told the Colossians that their hope was contained in "the word of the truth, the gospel that has come to you" (Colossians 1:5-6). What exactly is the gospel they heard? If we look closely at the rest of the epistle to the Colossians, we discover that the gospel is best told in story form. The gospel is a metanarrative, that is, a dominant story that has the power to transform. The Christian metanarrative has four basic parts to it: death, resurrection, ascension and return. It is the story of Jesus and also our story.

We are grafted into Jesus' story. And we are unified by the story. I want to unpack the four elements of the story and show how each part draws us into the larger narrative. Notice how each of these four verses in Colossians tells about Jesus and what he did, but also includes us in his story.

1. Death. "You have died, and your life is hidden with Christ in God" (Colossians 3:3).

Jesus died on the cross. This we all know. But the fact that we, by faith, participate in that death is not often taught, even though it is mentioned in many of Paul's letters. Paul is reminding the Colossians that they have died and that their life is hidden with Christ. Though they were not on the cross with him, they participate vicariously in his death. In another sense, they *have* died. Their old way of life ended. They have died to the narratives that once controlled them, the ones told in the kingdoms of this world, the ones that tell us "might makes right" and "money gives you joy" and "sex is the way to fulfillment." Those old idols have been smashed by the Christ narrative, and we enter into that story.

Before I came into a living relationship of love and trust with the Trinity, I was living for myself and was guided by the principalities and powers of this world. When I gave my life to Jesus the "old Jim" died. But a new Jim emerged, and that new life is largely unseen to me because it is "hidden with Christ in God." For now I live by faith and am caught up in the story of Jesus. Jesus invites us to die, not on a cross but to ourselves (Luke 9:23). The old way of life, built on competition and vanity, dies with Jesus. What emerges is a new life, hidden from us, but no doubt real, safe and secure. It is our true self.

2. Resurrection. "When you were buried with him in baptism, you were also raised with him through faith in the power of God, who raised him from the dead" (Colossians 2:12).

Many Christians are not aware that they also participate in the *resurrection* of Jesus. The same power that raised Jesus from the dead also lives in us. The old you and me were dead, but the new you and me have been raised. Elsewhere Paul wrote, "So if anyone is in Christ, there is a new creation: everything old has passed away; see, everything has become new!" (2 Corinthians 5:17). We are new people, in whom Christ dwells. This awareness not only gives me strength as an individual, but it binds me together with other Christ-followers. In Brazil I felt very alien due to the language and cultural barriers. But when I went to church there and we began to sing, I knew I was home. I was with sisters and brothers who had died and risen with Christ, just as I have.

There emerges a new me, a new self, established by Christ. We have put on a new self (Colossians 3:10), which is being renewed constantly. I have a new identity: one in whom Christ dwells and delights. This is not my doing; it is by the power of God, the same power that raised Jesus from the tomb. I go forth in that power each day, as one who died but has been reborn. Jesus' resurrection is also my resurrection. That is my new story.

3. Ascension. "Set your hearts on things above, where Christ is seated at the right hand of God" (Colossians 3:1 NIV).

Jesus died and rose again, and then *ascended.* Some people think the ascension of Jesus was the day Jesus flew away, never to be seen again. In fact, the ascension of Jesus is an important part of the story. Jesus is now enthroned as the supreme Lord of all. Jesus now reigns, and one day every knee will bow and every tongue will confess that Jesus is Lord. Paul tells the Colossians to set their hearts on things above, which he explains is "where Christ is seated at the right hand of God." Notice that Jesus is *seated.* That is because his work is complete. To set our minds and hearts on "things above" means to focus on the finished work of Jesus, the source of our hope and strength. We find our unity in that common vision.

We are called to set our hearts on the victory established by Jesus.

Walter Brueggemann notes that this victory, like our new life, is often hidden from us, which is why we need to work hard to see it in our midst.

> The victory of God in our time over this deathly idolatry is hidden from us, as God's decisive victory is always hidden from us. We do not know exactly when and where the victory has been wrought. It is hidden in the weakness of neighbor love, in the foolishness of mercy, in the vulnerability of compassion, in the staggering alternatives of forgiveness and generosity which permit new life to emerge in situations of despair and brutality.

Jesus defeated the things that oppress us, which is the reason for our hope. It is not flashed by neon signs but is still all around us. We see it when a neighbor serves another and when people forgive or extend hospitality or generosity. When we do this, we are participating in the victory of Jesus.

4. Return. "When Christ who is your life is revealed, then you also will be revealed with him in glory" (Colossians 3:4).

The final part of the story has not yet occurred. The church proclaims, "Christ has died. Christ is risen. Christ will come again." The return of Jesus is the promise of ultimate healing and justice. All of the wrongs will be made right, all of the pain will end, and our joy will be made complete when Jesus comes in final victory. That hope binds the Christian community together as we await the final consummation of this divine conspiracy.

THE STORY BECOMES OUR STORY

We are members of Christ and of the kingdom of God because we have entered into the larger story of Jesus. This is not merely to make us feel special or secure (though it certainly does); it should also lead to a change in behavior. The story creates a new identity, which in turn leads to new practices. Jesus' story becomes my story; I am then *in Christ*, and as one indwelt by Christ my behavior begins to change.

I am not perfect, and I will struggle with the "old Jim," who was and is influenced by American culture, narratives and values. But the key is that identity comes before behavior. We almost always do the reverse: we define identity on the basis of behavior; we tell people

what they must do (imperative) to find out who they are (indicative). Paul does the opposite: he tells them who they are and then how they should live. The more we grow into the story, the more the story grows into us. Stanley Hauerwas, who is a Christian pacifist, con-

> "Identity comes before behavior." Journal about how you perceive the relationship between identity and behavior.

fesses in his great book *The Peaceable Kingdom:* "My wholeness, my integrity, is made possible by the truthfulness of the story. . . . Only by growing into the story do I learn how much violence I have stored in my soul, a violence which is not about to vanish overnight, but which I must continually work to recognize and lay down." I appreciate his honesty, and I relate to it. As we grow into the story, as he puts it, the integrity of the story clashes with our lack of integrity. When William Penn began growing into the Christ story, the elitism stored in his soul became unsettling. He wore the sword as long as he could or as long as his story-shaped soul could handle it

For Hauerwas the story and the new identity unearthed the violence stored in his soul; for Penn it was his pride. It will be different for each of us, but the point is that the integrity of the story remains true. The main point is that the story, and the identity it creates, must take the lead in changing our behavior and not the reverse, which is so common. In this world we determine identity on the basis of behavior, which leads to frustration and legalism. Again, Hauerwas explains it well: "The question 'What ought I to be?' precedes the question 'What ought I to do?'" The order is crucial. The indicative (who we are) must precede the imperative (how we should live). To understand who we are, we have to realize that we are a people whose roots are from another world. That is precisely why we are so peculiar.

HOPE IN ACTION

The often-quoted dictum attributed to Saint Francis is certainly true: "Preach the gospel wherever you go. When necessary, use words." Our lives are preaching all of the time. This can be an intimidating thought, especially on those bad days when we grumble and whine.

> What changes have you seen in your narratives and your story?

While we are not called to be perfect, we are called to be a witness to the larger story that has produced hope in us. Faith and love spring from hope. Let me explain how that works and then offer some examples of how we might improve our witness through our actions. The key, however, is remembering who we are (one in whom Christ dwells), where we live (in the unshakable kingdom of God) and to what we are destined (eternal glory with Jesus).

When I get out of bed tomorrow morning, I will arise with the sense that I am okay. More than okay, actually. The world around me, the one I step into when I leave my house, will tell me that my value and my worth are found in my abilities or performance. But I know better now. I have died to that old way. And I have risen with Jesus, who lives in me and loves me (Galatians 2:20). In other words, I am safe and secure. The old me that needs to compete, to impress, to dominate and to control has died. I am putting on the new self, which is being renewed in knowledge according to the image of Jesus (Colossians 3:10). So I don't need to worry today, for example. I am at peace, because my life is securely hidden in Christ (Colossians 3:3). So I will set my mind and heart on the victory of Jesus, my Lord and King and Teacher, who has created me for something wonderful.

I once asked the legendary basketball coach—and wise witness to Jesus—John Wooden what he thinks about as he begins each day. He said, "I have this one thought: Make today a masterpiece." That is the opportunity each of us has each day. We can make this day a masterpiece, something beautiful, extraordinary, magnificent and certainly peculiar. What exactly would that look like? In Paul's epistle to the Romans he lists a number of ways we can demonstrate our hope in our relationships with one another:

> Be devoted to one another in brotherly love. Honor one another above yourselves. Never be lacking in zeal, but keep your spiritual fervor, serving the Lord. Be joyful in hope, patient in affliction, faithful in prayer. Share with God's people who are in need. Practice hospitality.
>
> Bless those who persecute you; bless and do not curse. Rejoice with those who rejoice; mourn with those who mourn. Live in harmony with one another. Do not be proud, but be willing to associate with people of low position. Do not be conceited.
>
> Do not repay anyone evil for evil. Be careful to do what is right in the eyes of everybody. If it is possible, as far as it depends on you, live at peace with everyone. (Romans 12:10-18 NIV)

This is one of my favorite sections in the Bible. It paints a picture of how we preach the gospel without words. What might that look like in a normal life? And what does it have to do with hope?

Today a friend of mine shared with me some difficult news. I listened carefully, and let him know that I am with him through this trial. He does the same for me, for we are "devoted to one another," as Paul said. We don't need to proclaim it; you could see it when we bowed our heads and prayed. We were able to laugh, even in the pain, because we are "joyful in hope."

On Sunday our church invited people to stay after the service and fill boxes of food and clothing for the Haitian people, who had been devastated by a recent earthquake. They were "[sharing] with God's people who are in need." Two of my friends have begun befriending people at the homeless shelter. My friends have good jobs and good incomes and are highly educated, but in establishing these friendships they are "willing to associate with people of low position." Not out of pity but out of love.

Remember the wisdom of Dallas Willard: "The true social activist is the person who lives as an apprentice of Jesus in his or her ordinary relationships." It means living with a kingdom mind and heart in our marriages, with our parents and our children, with our coworkers, our neighbors and the guy at the hardware store who is blocking the aisle.

> "Be joyful in hope, patient in affliction, faithful in prayer. Share with God's people who are in need. Practice hospitality." How have you seen these signs of community at work in your church or fellowship group?

The new self lives in new ways, and this is seen—and smelled—by those around us. Paul said to the Corinthians, "We are the aroma of Christ to God among those who are being saved and among those who are perishing" (2 Corinthians 2:15). But the aroma of Christ is not a cologne or perfume you can buy at the mall. There is no "Eau de Jesus" aftershave. However, when we tell the truth when it is hard, when we sit in the waiting room with a hurting and scared friend when we have pressing things to do, when we strive to stay in harmony with people who disagree with us, when we find a way to spend less so we can give more, when we offer a blessing to someone who curses at us, the essence of Jesus, who lives in and through us, is emerging.

I once ate, without knowing it, eight garlic cloves. I thought they were little, tasty potatoes sautéed in butter. When I got home that night and got in bed, the odor I was exuding was so strong that my wife shot up and said, "What did you eat?" "Some roast beef and little buttery potatoes," I answered. "No, you ate garlic. Those little potatoes were garlic cloves." I ended up sleeping on the couch. The next day I brushed my teeth twice, rinsed with mouthwash and chewed gum. During church she leaned over and said, "You still smell like garlic." The problem was that it was in my system, in my blood and in my lungs, and coming out of my pores. I think of that story when I think about being the aroma of Christ. When we know and live and breathe the truth that we are people indwelt by Christ, the reality of Jesus is in our lungs and on our lips and in our pores. We cannot help it. Fortunately, unlike garlic, when people catch the scent of Jesus on us—through our actions—they don't ask us to move away. They usually want to know the reason for our hope.

HOPE IN WORDS

While our actions speak the loudest, we are also called on to share the gospel of hope in words. Peter wrote to the early Christians, "Always be ready to make your defense to anyone who demands from you an accounting for the hope that is in you; yet do it with gentleness and reverence" (1 Peter 3:15-16).

There is a lot of wisdom in this verse. First, Peter encourages us to be prepared. This assumes that we have spent some time thinking about the four-part story and reflecting on how to share that story if and when it is needed. I love the next phrase: *an accounting for the hope that is in you.* That is all people really need to hear. They don't want a lengthy explanation about the authority of the Bible or why the Muslims are wrong. They just want to know what happened to you, how you got caught up in a new story and a new set of practices.

The last phrase is also a gem: *do it with gentleness and reverence.* Far too often people share their faith with harshness and condescension. Some Christians act like arrogant bullies when they evangelize, and it is always counterproductive. How do we give the reason for our hope with *gentleness* and *reverence?* By telling our story. It is difficult to argue with your story, and no one but you can tell that story. It is the story of your own life, how you became aware of the larger story of Jesus and how your life was written into that story, so that

Jesus' story is now your story as well. That is the gentle way. The respectful way is to do so only when people are interested. Timing is important. In addition to being gentle, we also need to be patient. Jesus told his disciples, "Behold, I send you forth as sheep in the midst of wolves: be ye therefore wise as serpents, and harmless as doves" (Matthew 10:16 KJV).

Dallas Willard once quoted this verse and then asked me, "What is the 'wisdom of the serpent'?" I had actually never thought about it, though I knew the verse well, even in the King James Version that Dallas had practically memorized. "Well, have you ever seen a snake chase someone?" I answered no. He said, "That is because the wisdom of the serpent is to wait until someone comes to them."

Of course, we are not trying to kill or bite anyone, which is why Jesus adds being harmless as doves. Doves are about as harmless as you can get. They are even symbols of peace. When we combine the wisdom of the serpent and gentleness of the dove, we have found the right approach to evangelism. Frank Laubach waited nearly a year before

> What responses are stirred in you as you read Frank Laubach's story?

speaking to the people he had come to evangelize in the Philippines. He simply did his work faithfully and kept his mind on things above. In time the Muslim leaders told the people, "Go spend time with that man. He knows God." He waited and was gentle. He also respected the people and cared for them by teaching them how to read. Laubach was a man of hope, and from that hope sprang faith and love.

GETTING HOPE

My wife and I both teach, but on different sides of town. Each day at 4:10 p.m. I pick up my daughter, Hope at her elementary school. I leave the university a few minutes before 4:00, and on my way out I usually see three or four people who know me. They will say, "Headin' out for the day?" and I reply, "Yeah, I have to go get Hope." Each

time I say that I smile. I have to get Hope. On one level that is true. I
am going to pick up a little girl by that name. On another level it is
also true. She is the embodiment of hope for my wife and me, a living
reminder that God is worth trusting, which is why we named her
Hope in the first place. On another level it is also true that I am going
to get hope because hope is what I live by. It is where my roots are
planted. But in another sense it is entirely not true. I don't get hope;
hope has gotten ahold of me. Every day I get a chance to make a masterpiece, each brushstroke of faith and love witnessing to the God
who overcame death and in his great mercy offers that eternal life to
you and to me. That hope is alive and will never die.

> Blessed be the God and Father of our Lord Jesus Christ! By his
> great mercy he has given us a new birth into a living *hope* through
> the resurrection of Jesus Christ from the dead. (1 Peter 1:3)

sharing your faith
(without embarrassment or coercion)

Who should you witness to? What are the criteria in deciding who to share your faith with and when to share it? And finally, how do we go about it? As noted in this chapter, we are always witnessing, whether we know it or not. People are watching us, and our actions communicate something, for good or for ill. Having said that, I want to offer an exercise that will help us when we become more intentional about reaching out to others and drawing them into the life of faith. There are seven activities I have found helpful in the process, some of which will look different depending on our current relationship with the person we are witnessing to. If we know the person well, and he or she already trusts us, we can move more quickly through the process, even jumping all the way to the last act. Still, all of the previous parts are necessary because they remind us that we are not doing this alone but are relying on God at every juncture.

1. PRAY

The first thing we can do is pray for God to send us someone. This is a powerful prayer that nearly always gets answered, and soon. The Holy Spirit is far wiser and more knowledgeable than we are. He knows the needs of those we know. Pray not only for God to send those people your way, pray also that you would have eyes and ears to know it when they come. Perhaps there is a person who is already on your heart. Pray for that person and for God to create an opportunity to take a step toward faith sharing.

2. WATCH
Once you have prayed, keep watch. Ask God regularly, "Help me see who you are bringing me. Give me eyes of compassion. Let me know who it is and when I can take the next step." Remember the wisdom of the serpent.

3. REACH OUT
Once you have a sense about who that person is and have sensed God preparing the relationship, find ways to reach out to the person in nonthreatening ways. Ask him or her to have coffee or to go to lunch. If this person is already someone you spend time with, reach out by asking nonthreatening yet searching questions, such as "How are you feeling about life right now? What is working? What is missing?" If you do not know the person well, these questions will be too personal. Keep the conversation at a more basic level, but keep listening for clues to their heart.

4. LISTEN
Listen well. This is so seldom done in our harried and hurried culture that it almost seems like a lost skill. Simply by listening you are demonstrating love. Listen for clues to the condition of the person's heart. What is he or she longing for? Struggling with? The best thing to ask yourself privately is, "Where do I think God is working in this person's life?" It may be healing from a divorce, the joy of a new job or the grief of losing a loved one. Whatever it is, try to discover what the person cares about.

5. CONNECT
It is at this stage that your understanding of the gospel (our God

reigns and our God is with us) comes into play. If you have discerned what is pressing on the person's heart, try to connect his or her situation with the message of the gospel. Let's say you sense that a friend is struggling with grief over the loss of a loved one. Ask yourself, *How does the gospel apply to her (or his) situation?* There are many ways, but three come to mind: first, Jesus defeated death; second, God stands with us in our darkness; and third, God can do great things through our pain.

If the relationship is strong enough to bear it, you may want to make those connections verbally by asking questions such as, "What is giving you hope right now? What keeps you going?" If the person is open, you will probably get a long answer. Try to continue making connections between the person's condition and the good news you know, without preaching. You are in a dialogue at this stage. At some point you might be able to more explicitly draw the connection between what is happening in his or her life and what God has done and will do.

6. SHARE

At some point you might be asked to tell your story or share your thoughts. If that happens, do not be afraid. There are some false narratives that prevent people from sharing their faith.

While each of these is worth examining, let me simply say this: God is not asking us to be perfect or have all of the answers. God is asking us to invite people into an interactive life with the Trinity. The kingdom is not in trouble, as I like to say. It does not need a PR expert. The kingdom is just waiting for people to give it a chance. Please forgive my nonpastoral tone, but I would simply say, "Get over it. Let go of your inhibitions."

Remember Peter's advice: "Always be ready to make your defense to anyone who demands from you an accounting for the hope that is in you; yet do it with gentleness and reverence" (1 Peter 3:15-16).

What I love about this verse is that it does not say, "You must go

to seminary and study systematic theology, church history, apologet-
ics and philosophy. Only then will you be fit to witness." It simply
says, "Be prepared to tell people why you have hope—and do it with
gentleness and respect."

This means explaining how the message of the gospel has inter-
sected your life. This is not a time to explain. Just tell your story,
how you came to know God, how God has been at work in your life.
Be honest. Let the person know that you are not perfect, that you
have struggled, but you nonetheless have put your confidence in
God. One way to help you do this is to memorize the verses from
Colossians in the section of this chapter titled "The Four-Part Story
of Hope." The more you become familiar with that four-part story
and how it is your story, the more you will be able to articulate your
message of hope.

7. INVITE

At a certain point in your relationship, invite the person to join with
you and other Christ-followers in some capacity. It may be in church.
This is usually not very threatening, but it can be for some. You might
want to invite him or her to spend time with you and some of your
Christian friends in a social setting (dinner or a movie), and perhaps
even a small group Bible study. Some people find it less threatening
to be with a group of five or six in a home than in a church with five
hundred strangers. Another idea is to invite your friend to join you
and other apprentices in a service project. This can be a powerful
witness.

Above all, keep praying for this person. And be prepared for it to
take time. The average time between when someone first begins
seeking and when he or she actually makes a commitment of faith is
twenty-eight months. At a certain point you should invite the person
to church or help him or her find a church. Though we may experience a key moment we call conversion, in truth we go through many
conversions and develop new facets of our life with God, and the

church is the only place that can do this. Finally, trust God. The journey this person is on will have twists and turns you and I could never imagine, just as mine did. God will bring the right people at the right time. For now, you are privileged to be one person on that journey, telling your story and pointing your friend to the God who reigns.

three

The serving community

I once asked a pastor, "If the life of discipleship to Jesus really takes root in a community of people, particularly in a local church, how would you know if it was really beginning to make a difference?" Without hesitation he said, "In committee meetings." My first response was to chuckle, because I know, from many years on church committees, just how discouraging they can be and how badly people can behave. I was a bit surprised at his answer, though I might have thought he would say, "They would be more engaged in worship," or "They carry their Bibles everywhere," or even "They sign up for more community service." The pastor went on to tell me that the problem in many church committee meetings is that the people walk in with two ways of thinking. Some of the members realize the work being done is for God, for the good of the people, to make the world better, to advance the kingdom of God. But others are more influenced by the values and goals that run the kingdom of this world. I asked him for an example.

"We were having a trustees meeting one evening, and our primary issue was over the new building we were planning on adding to our campus. This was something the people on the committee had very strong feelings about, caused by two concerns. One concern was that we had hit a place where we had not been growing numerically, and it may have been caused by the fact that we simply had no space. We were packed in all of our services, and we really needed more room. The second reason we were not growing, some suspected, was that a church just up the road had recently experienced a lot of growth—which included members from our church who had joined their congregation—and some on the committee felt that it was because they had a better facility than ours."

The pastor went on, "The discussion turned to one of the members of the committee, an architect, who had been working on the blueprint for the new building. They asked him questions about what the building would be like, how much it would cost and how many people it would hold. At one point a person, who probably meant well but phrased the question poorly, asked him, 'What I want to know is this: Can we build a building that will help us compete with the church down the road?' The architect paused and said, 'Give me a second,' and he took a deep breath and went on to say, 'I needed to think for a minute whether I was going to answer that question from inside or outside of the kingdom of God.' "

> Have you ever had to pause and reflect on whether you were participating in the kingdom of God in your answer or actions?

The fact that he had to pause to think about how to answer revealed that the two ways of thinking, two different narratives, were in the room. One was built upon worldly values, such as competition, success in terms of numbers and self-preservation. The other was rooted in the kingdom of God, a place of cooperation, success in terms of service and self-sacrifice. Those two narratives often clash in church committee meetings, the pastor noted, because the members are shaped by two different stories. When someone begins to tune in to the kingdom-of-God narratives in his or her life, and has been working to apply them, you will see it most clearly in the way they behave in church committee meetings. I told the pastor, "So then, the best argument for helping people grow in their discipleship to Jesus is not just for the sake of their souls but for the improvement of committee meetings." We both laughed, but in fact we had touched on a deep truth.

FALSE NARRATIVE: OUR NEEDS MATTER THE MOST

The architect in the story was in a position that all apprentices of Jesus find themselves in on a regular basis. Each day we make thousands of decisions, and while many of them have little effect on our souls ("Should I wear brown or black pants today?"), there are many decisions that expose the state of our souls. The question posed to the architect was one of those soul-exposing questions. Behind either answer we give lies a narrative. We have been shaped much by the narratives of this world, and it is difficult to shed them. One of the most dominant narratives is built on self-preservation, personal happiness and making sure our needs are met. This narrative is not only for individuals. It can also be the foundation for a community.

The church committee meeting was composed of people who had one thing in common: they were members of a specific community. The community provides them many things: a home, a common vision and, over time, a history of great memories. People love their communities. We become protective of them and want to see them succeed. The church committee in the opening story consisted of people who are giving their time and energy to help the church do well. There is nothing wrong with loving the community of Christ-followers who have nurtured you and perhaps your family for many years. And there is nothing wrong with wanting things to go well with your church and its ministry. There is nothing wrong, for example, with being concerned about how to make sure the pastor gets paid each month or that the parking lot is sufficient.

The problem comes when the most important consideration, the dominant desire and the main focus of a community is its own success. Just as an individual whose whole life is focused on meeting his or her own needs becomes narcissistic, self-centered, ineffective and ultimately unhappy, so also communities can become so focused on themselves that they lose their souls. When that happens, the larger vision, the one that brought the community into existence, has been eclipsed, and the community no longer exists to fulfill its original mission but simply to stay alive. This is often the first step toward spiritual death and, ultimately, the demise of the community.

In my early days as the chaplain of Friends University, I was privileged to work with about a hundred college students who participated in the various ministries on campus, from a weekly fellowship gathering to retreats, small groups and mission work. I was the spiritual leader for these young people; they trusted me and often followed my lead. I got a call from a local pastor who asked me to lunch. He told me that his church had held a meeting and wanted to offer several thousand dollars to our campus ministry program. I was elated as I thought about what this money could do for our students. Then the pastor said, "All we are asking is that you teach a Sunday school class for young people." I agreed, and not long after there were about twenty-five students from the college who came to the class. Everything seemed to be going well.

> Give an example of a time you have seen a community lose its focus. What was the result?

Then I got a call from the pastor a month later. "Jim," he said, "we have a problem. Your college students are not attending our worship service. They are coming to your class and then leaving, either going to other churches or just going home." I was surprised to hear that. I was not aware of this problem as I myself also left to worship at our home church with my family. The pastor went on, "If you are not going to get your kids in worship, then we are not going to fund your ministry any longer." I asked some of the students in the Sunday school class why they did not want to worship in the church where we met—especially those who had no other church home. They all said the same thing: "It is boring. There is no one under fifty. No one even talks to us. So we stopped going." I could not force them to go, and soon I stopped teaching and the money was no longer given. Unfortunately, this church was focusing on its needs, not the students' needs.

TRUE NARRATIVE:
OTHERS' NEEDS MATTER THE MOST

In contrast, the following year I got a call from a layleader at another local church who said, "Jim, our church has been praying a lot, and we feel that we have a lot to offer young people. We are an older congregation, and not very large, but we have a lot of wisdom, and we care about the next generation. We know you work with college students, and we want to ask you to help us find out how to minister to them." Over the next few months I met with the people at this church. They had no money to offer. They simply wanted to know what college students need in a home church.

I told them that first, they like to eat. They are used to having no money, and the cafeteria in those days was not open on Sundays. The people at the church said, "We are good at food." Second, the students who are from out of state often miss their families. They could use a warm hug and a sense of being welcomed. The church folks said, "We are good at hugging." I concluded, "I think that is about it." Then one older lady said, "Will they like our worship style, Jim? We don't have any guitars, just an organ, and we sing hymns." I said, "If you love them and feed them, I don't think they will mind. They are not as interested in being entertained as people think they are."

I invited about a half-dozen students to attend the church with me. There was a lot of hugging when we came in the door. The worship service was a traditional one, with hymns and Scripture reading, some liturgy, a sermon and Communion. The pastor had a great heart and offered a solid message. I could tell that the students felt at home. There was nothing hip or cool about it, but they got plenty of hip and cool during the rest of the week. After the service, we went to the fellowship hall. The ladies of the church had made a feast, complete with the mandatory green bean casserole and Jell-O with fruit inside. The students loved it. So did I. In fact, I never left that church. It was such an others-minded congregation that, a few years later, they decided to end the ministry they had in that part of town to form a new congregation, which became Chapel Hill United Methodist Church, where I still attend.

What was the difference between the two churches? The first church was asking the question, What can we do to improve our church? The second church was asking, How can we serve others? The first church was operating from a narrative of *self-focus*. The second church was operating from a narrative of *focusing on others*. The first church cared only about its own image and its own preservation; having college students attend their church was a sign of success. The second church cared only about the well-being of the students; having college students in their midst was an opportunity to serve. When we are steeped in the reality of the kingdom, our focus shifts from our needs to the needs of others. It is only possible when we are caught up in the kingdom of God. Only then, when we are confident and secure, can we shift our focus away from ourselves and onto others.

> In your community, how have you grappled with these questions of how to improve your church and/or how to serve others?

THE OTHERS-CENTERED COMMUNITY
The good and beautiful community of Jesus finds its life and power in Jesus himself, who is not only our teacher but also our source of

strength. As Jesus is, so are his followers. Jesus was a servant. He lived for the good of others. In the kingdom of this world, greatness is defined by power. The one who is served is greater than the one who serves. Jesus reversed this notion of greatness: "Who is greater, the one who is at the table or the one who serves? Is it not the one at the table? But I am among you as one who serves" (Luke 22:27).

His example becomes our example. Not merely because we want to imitate him and perhaps earn his favor. Being a servant of others is the highest way to live. Wanting and needing to be served by others is not life-producing but soul-destroying. Jesus showed us that by example. Jesus, the Creator of the universe, the King of all things, comes to serve. He washes the feet of the disciples. He lives to serve.

This is because he was and is moved by one thing: love. He told his disciples that the greatest expression of love is to give of yourself for the good of others. In fact, the greatest act of love would be to offer your life in exchange for the well-being of another should you be in a position do so. Jesus said, "No one has greater love than this, to lay down one's life for one's friends" (John 15:13).

He not only taught it, he lived it. He gave his life for the good of others, including you and me. We who follow him as teacher are called on to do the same, to shift our focus away from ourselves and onto others.

How can we do this? How was the second church able to do this, whereas the first church was not? The solution is found in the kingdom of God. As noted in chapter two, faith and love spring from the hope that we discover in the gospel proclamation. In that good news we discover, as Julian of Norwich noted, that all is well and all manner of things shall be well. We have confidence in a great future; we know that nothing will happen to us that God, in his wisdom, has not allowed, and that he cannot use for good. We are safe and secure. In that condition, we can move from self-focus to focusing on others.

When we live with Jesus in his kingdom our basic needs are met—even if it takes other Christians to provide them. In the kingdom we are given the material provision we need (even if we do not have shelter, food and clothing, there are organizations that can provide them—they are usually organizations that serve as outposts of the kingdom and are run predominantly by apprentices of Jesus). In the kingdom of God we are safe and secure. Not even death can separate us from the love of God. In the kingdom of God we discover that we are loved, forever, and without condition. In the kingdom of God we also learn that we are valuable and precious, worth dying for. As Eugene Peterson says, we are "splendid, never-to-be-duplicated stories of grace."

When we appropriate these truths, we are able to turn our attention to others and their needs. The first church, I later discovered, was living in fear. Though they had a lot of money, they were aging quickly, and with no new people coming in to the church, they faced the possibility of closing their doors. They confused the life of their church with the kingdom of God. Churches come and go, but the kingdom is eternal. Their life, power and reason for existence are in the kingdom of God, and it will never falter. The second church knew this instinctively. Even though they loved their little church and could wax nostalgic about their history, they were also ready to move on if needed, which in fact they did. Out of the death of that church came new life.

> Do you agree with the idea that a church may close its doors, but the kingdom is eternal? Why or why not?

Communities become others-centered when they are steeped in the narrative of the kingdom of God. They know that their community is an outpost of the kingdom of God, a place where grace is spoken and lived for as long as is needed. The value of a church is not in its longevity but in its love. The success of a church is not in its size but in its service to the people and the community. We are a people founded by a person who never established a church or built a building or led a finance campaign to build impressive buildings. Our leader just came and served and then died for the good of others. I suppose that would be a pretty good mission statement for a church, but one I am not likely to see: "We exist to serve others and then die, just like our Founder."

TREASURING OUR TREASURES

Paul told the community at Philippi how to live with one another in day to day life: "Do nothing out of selfish ambition or vain conceit, but in humility consider others better than yourselves. Each of you should look not only to your own interests, but also to the interests of others" (Philippians 2:3-4 NIV). I once taught a class using this verse as the main text, and a woman raised her hand and said, "I don't think that is very good psychology on Paul's part—to 'consider others better than yourselves.' That is just bad self-esteem." What she failed to understand, I believe, is that it is possible to have a high regard for others and a proper self-image at the same time. She assumed that to think of others as better meant to think badly of yourself.

The problem arises because we are not used to thinking of someone as "better" than ourselves. Notice also that in the second verse Paul encourages them to "look not only to your own interests, but also to the interests of others" (v. 4). He knows that we are naturally going to look to our own interests, and he does not say that is bad. He is just asking us to look out for the interests of others as well. The best way for me to grasp what Paul is saying, and to live it out, came to me a couple of years ago while I was writing a sermon I was going to give for a wedding. I thought about what has helped my own marriage. I thought about how amazing and wonderful my wife, Meghan, is, and I scribbled down the world *treasure*. To me, she is a precious treasure. Then a thought came to me: *Treasure your treasure.*

My wife is a great gift to me, a person of sacred worth. When I set my mind and heart on that reality, it is easy for me to treasure her, to love her, to look out for her well-being and to sacrifice my own desires at times in order to care for hers. My children are also sacred and wonderful treasures. Sometimes I forget that and find caring for them a chore. Then I remember, and suddenly caring for them is less a duty and more of a privilege. It is a matter of seeing, seeing the beauty and worth of a person, that increases our desire to serve. "O God, help me believe the truth about myself—no matter how beautiful it is," wrote Macrina Wiederkehr.

> When you think of "treasuring your treasure," what people come to mind?

While there is certainly truth in her prayer, I like to change the wording: "O God, help me see the truth about those I meet today—no matter how beautiful they are."

OTHERS-MINDED EVEN WHEN IT HURTS

The core narrative we choose to live by will determine our behavior—my needs first or your needs first. A friend told me about something that happened to her recently. She runs in social circles with a non-Christian woman with whom she has tried to establish a friendship. She has invited this woman to lunch on several occasions, but the woman has always had an excuse for being unable to meet with her. She tried several times to invite her by calling the woman's secretary. The secretary, feeling badly, finally said, "I may be out of line, but the last time I wrote a note to her with your lunch request on it, she took it, wadded it up and said, 'That is never gonna happen,' as she tossed it in the trash. You are a nice person, and I don't want you to keep getting treated this way."

My friend said she was hurt by this story, as we all would be. But she lives deeply in the kingdom and turned the matter over to God in prayer. About a week later she happened to be in a restaurant, and the woman came in with a friend. She told her waiter, "I would like to pay for their check when they are done." She was busy completing some paperwork she had brought with her but looked up to see the woman standing in front of her.

"I just wanted to say thank you for buying our lunch. That was very kind," the woman said. "I know you have been persistent in trying to meet with me. I am sorry. I want you to know that."

My friend explained her action to me this way. She said, "You know, I don't expect that we will get together any time soon, but that was not why I did it. I bought her lunch because I have been praying for her, and I had a chance to do something nice for her. I think God gave me that opportunity. Whether or not we become friends and God uses me to reach her, I don't know. All I know is that I had a chance to do something for someone else, and it felt good to be able to do it." She is living by a new, strong, true narrative: "Your needs are what matters most." She is peculiar indeed.

Now there's one caveat to all this: Though many of us, myself included, do not run the risk of overserving or being too concerned with the needs of others to the neglect of our own, there are many people who are—and those kinds of people are also likely to read a book like this one. We need to have balance when it comes to the issue of serving others and taking care of ourselves. I have many Christian friends who are so focused on serving others that they neglect their own needs, and sometimes the needs of their families. One woman confessed that she had burned out and left the church when she was younger because she had been told that serving others was our constant duty as Christ-followers. So she did and found herself worn-out and discouraged. Another man shared that for many years his own family "only got my leftovers," because "I spent all of my energy caring for people in need and neglected them."

I encourage balance when it comes to serving others. We need to be aware of the condition of our own souls and bodies, and to take care of that first, without feeling any guilt about it. We can only

give when we are grounded and rested. We also need to be mindful
that some of the people who need us the most are those we seldom
give our time to, which is often our families and friends. They may
not be in a condition of great need, but they need our time, energy
and love. Again, we need to find balance. It is possible to spend too
much time caring for our own needs, and it is common to see people spending too much time caring for the needs of others. I believe
we can strike the right balance if we listen to the leading of the
Spirit and are open to the discernment of others who can see things
we may not see.

THE MOST IMPORTANT JOB

I was once with Dallas Willard, speaking at a conference in Califor-
nia. I opened the evening session with a talk about God's grace in
human transformation. After a break, Dallas got up to speak. He
opened with these attention-catching words: "I am going to tell you
what is the single most important task of a Christian, especially
those who are in church leadership." There was a moment of silence
as we waited to hear what he believed was *the most important task* of
a Christian. My mind raced for a moment—what could it be? I have
heard Dallas teach for hundreds of hours. I thought he might say
"Scripture memorization," because I know he believes it is very
transforming. He leaned in to the microphone and said, "The most
important task we have, especially for those in church leadership, is
to pray for the success of our neighboring churches."

I was stunned. The most important task? I could easily come up
with a dozen things I would assume were far more important for
Christians, especially pastors. What about caring for the poor? What
about spending quality time with God in solitude and prayer? What
about sharing our faith with nonbelievers? No, according to Dallas,
the most important thing we can do is to pray for the success and
well-being of the other churches in our area. I pressed Dallas later to
explain what he meant. He said that when we pray, genuinely pray,

for the success of the churches that are in our proximity, we are breaking the narrative of selfishness and entering into the mind of God, who is also praying for the success of those churches. The practice, he said, puts us in sync with the kingdom of God.

He encouraged not only pastors but entire churches to do this. Recently I was preaching at Highland Park Community Church in Casper, Wyoming, and the pastor did just that. He listed a few churches in the area and asked God to bless the work of their hands. He named the churches and even mentioned some of the ministries within those churches. It was a beautiful thing. It changed the atmosphere of worship; it connected us to something larger than ourselves; it helped us see the beauty and power of the kingdom of God. I asked one of the pastors about this practice, and he told me they do it every Sunday. I told him about what Dallas had said.

> What do you think about Dallas Willard's choice of praying for other churches as the most important task of a Christian? How does it put us "in sync with the kingdom of God"?

I said, "You all are doing it! Keep it up." He blushed a little bit, but I wanted to affirm what he was doing and what it was communicating to the people.

THE SPACE OF GRACE

When the architect paused to think about his answer during the committee meeting, he was choosing to live out the true narrative found in the teaching of Jesus and in the Epistles. The narrative teaches us that in the kingdom of God we are not competing with anyone. The narrative that says we are competing with others—especially other churches—is a false, illusory, fragile narrative that moves us further from God and ourselves. The architect wisely sought a space of grace, as I call it, where he could distance himself from the false narrative and discern the truth he encountered in the narrative of Jesus.

He had a space of grace, a pause in which he was able to speak from a Christ-centered place. The key here is that we learn how to find those spaces of grace in which we examine the narrative we are going to adopt. It is a slow process. But if we continue to reboot our minds and stay with the substantive narrative of Jesus, we will move closer to God and to ourselves, and the fruit of the Spirit will begin to flow out of us. So how did the architect answer the question, "Can we build a building that will help us compete with the church down the road?" He said something like this:

> First, I just want to make it clear. We are not competing with the church down the road. We are all on the same team. Their growth is our growth, because we are all together in the kingdom of God. Second, our job is simple: we need to do the best job we can with the money God has provided for us. That means working hard to build a beautiful space that will honor God and be a blessing to the people who inhabit it. And that is what I am trying to do with the skills I have been given and the training that I have done.

I said to the minister who was presiding at the meeting, "So, how did the others in the group react to his answer?"

"That was the amazing part," he explained.

> His answer changed the tenor of the whole meeting. We had been focused on the wrong things, using the wrong standards. The dominant, false narrative of church success had been on people's minds, which is that churches are evaluated by the *ABCs*: attendance, building and cash. When that is our focus, everything goes wrong because those are not the values of the kingdom. I try to say the kind of things the architect said, but they often think, "Oh, that is just the preacher using preacher talk," but when he said it, it really spoke to them. The rest of the

meeting took a new direction. We started asking questions about how we could do the best job we can do with what God had given us. By the end of the meeting we were all excited to be a part of what God is doing in our midst.

The pastor concluded, "Changing the spirit of a church meeting from a worldly focus to a kingdom-of-God focus is no small feat. It was practically a miracle." As a veteran of many church meetings, I knew exactly what he meant.

Treasuring Our Treasures

The good and beautiful community of apprentices is made up of people learning how to put the needs of others ahead of their own. This is peculiar behavior in our world. It shows that we are maladjusted to the narratives of this world that tell us to "look out for number one" and that say "winning is not everything—it is the only thing." It shows that we are maladjusted to self-seeking, racism and aggression. How do we live this out? Where do we live this out? It begins, I think, by changing the way we see other people. If we see others— whether in our family or on the freeway—as merely human, it becomes easy to see them as either obstacles or opportunities to further our own happiness.

The key is to put on the mind of Christ and to see others as he sees them: treasures. Then we will naturally move to treasuring them, which makes putting their needs ahead of our own not only possible but likely. We live and move in different circles, and have different relationships with the people in our lives: family and friends, coworkers, fellow Christians, and strangers and acquaintances. It is easier, for example, to treasure my family, but that does not mean I do it well. It is harder to treasure the person who is being rude in the hardware store, but that does not mean it is impossible. This week I would like you to engage in several ways of treasuring the treasures all around us.

LIVING UNSELFISHLY AT HOME

1. When deciding where or what to eat, ask the others in your family where they would like to go. Unless the food they choose causes you to have an allergic reaction, go where they want to go, or eat what they want to eat.

2. If you are married or have a roommate, ask how the other person is doing, and really listen. Even if you have other things to do, practice putting his or her needs—even if it is an emotional need—ahead of yours.

3. If you have children in your home, give them the honor of choosing how to spend one evening this week—any way they want. It may be watching a movie or playing a board game, but the key is that they get to choose.

LIVING UNSELFISHLY AT WORK

1. Take time to visit a coworker and ask, "What are you working on that I might be able to help with or carry some of your burden?" This usually leads to some interesting requests!

2. Make coffee or tea for others, or bring some treats, or clean up the area where people get coffee and snacks.

LIVING UNSELFISHLY AT CHURCH

1. Park farther away from the sanctuary, rather than closer, to leave the space for others.

2. Sit up near the front of the sanctuary or in the spaces where people seldom sit, leaving room for others in the more desirable seats.

3. Offer to do some needed chores, such as folding bulletins or cleaning the parking lot.

LIVING UNSELFISHLY IN DAILY LIFE

1. When driving, be on the lookout for opportunities to let people in to your lane.

2. When shopping, be mindful of others as you navigate through the store, and allow others to cut ahead of you in line.

four

the christ-centered community

I got a call one day from a man who said he was one of the leaders of a denomination that I had heard of but frankly knew little about. He was calling on behalf of their leadership to see if I would come and speak to a group of denominational leaders on the topic of Christian spiritual formation. I was immediately interested. I asked how they got my name, and he said their denominational headquarters sent out a survey to several hundred laypeople in their churches asking what topics or subjects they would like to know more about. The number one answer was "spiritual formation." The man told me their denomination did not have anyone with expertise in this area, so they searched "spiritual formation" on the Internet and my name came up. (I had recently written a book titled *A Spiritual Formation Workbook*.)

He told me they needed to know more about this subject and that my time with them would ultimately have an effect on their churches. I accepted his invitation. For the next six months I worked hard and prayed a lot, asking God to help me ignite in these leaders a passion for Christian spiritual formation, as well as offer them guidance on how to make this happen in their churches.

As I flew to the meeting my excitement increased. I met a dear man at the baggage-claim area who drove me to the hotel where our daylong workshop was held. I went into the ballroom with my brief-case in hand, eager to begin teaching. The room was filled with over sixty key leaders from around the United States. *If these men can get a passion for this, their whole church could catch a new fire*, I thought to myself. One of the leaders of the denomination introduced me, and I stepped to the podium with energy. I shared a funny story, and the room seemed to relax. Then I launched into my main discussion and made the following statement: "God has offered us many different means of grace—prayer, solitude, silence, the Bible, fasting and many others—in order to deepen our relationship with God, and to de-velop the character of Christ so that we can live vibrant lives with God and make a difference in our world."

This was my well-crafted opening. It was also the end of my rap-port with this audience. I later learned that they ardently and fer-vently believe that God has given the church only *two* means of grace—baptism and Communion. All of the activities I mentioned (prayer, Bible reading, solitude) are not considered *means of grace*. My tradition (Methodism), and all of the others I had ever spoken to, freely uses that term to describe those activities. But I had never been informed about their position on this issue. All I knew was that the audience was quickly going from concerned to hostile.

I had almost no eye contact within a minute of that opening sen-tence. Within fifteen minutes I saw heads shaking in disagreement. Thirty minutes into the talk a man actually stood up, turned his chair around and sat with his back turned to me. He could have actually left the room (three men did that at about the forty-minute mark), but he wanted to make a public proclamation of his disgust. I had violated a sacred principle; I had unknowingly taken a theological position that was contrary to theirs. I was wrong, in their eyes, about the use of a phrase, and they needed to shame me publicly. I stopped at around fifty-five minutes and said, "It seems like a good time for a break."

During that break the man who had driven me from the airport said to me with a very sad face, "The president is very sorry, but he thinks this is going very badly, and that we need to end your time speaking." I was supposed to teach for the next four hours, but honestly, I wanted to go back in that room about as much as I wanted to walk into a hornet's nest. I knew I would feel the pain of this moment for years to come. I said to the

> Have you ever found yourself in a position where a miscommunication over theology created a seemingly insurmountable rift?

man, "I agree. Can you take me to the airport? Perhaps I can catch an early flight home." He said he would.

As I was walking down the lonely corridor I heard a voice. "Excuse me," a man whispered, "may I ask a question?" I said, "Sure." He said, "I am sorry about how you were treated. I am new to this denomination, recently ordained, and I don't share all of the same views as my fellow pastors. All I know is that I am unable to help my people grow in discipleship, and it seems you might be able to help me." His sincerity was clear, so I stopped to help. "Look," I said, "just do this. Read *Celebration of Discipline* by Richard Foster. You will have plenty to work on for many years. Read it for yourself and put it into practice in your own life first. In time you will change, and then you will naturally pass it on to your people." He thanked me, and I shuffled off, completely defeated, down the hallway to the parking lot. As I flew home, I leaned my head against the window and started to cry.

FALSE NARRATIVE:
IF WE DISAGREE, THEN WE MUST DIVIDE

I imagine many readers are now wondering, *Which denomination was that?* It doesn't matter. I suspect it could be any denomination, in that

similar stories happen all the time in churches. What I took away
from the experience was how something so small—three little
words—was the cause of such division. I take responsibility for not
being better prepared, which may have prevented the situation. But I
believe they were equally culpable for not extending grace to me for
my lack of knowledge. Someone should have interrupted me and said
something like, "Excuse me, Jim, but you just used a phrase that is a
bit charged for us. Here is our position on it . . ." and then offered me
a chance to respond.

Let me state the obvious and awful truth: the church of Jesus
Christ has been split into many different factions who refuse to have
fellowship with one another. For a people who claim one Lord, one
faith and one baptism, we are not one church but exist in isolation,
judgment, suspicion and condemnation. This is a sad and terrible
situation that undoubtedly grieves the Father, Son and Holy Spirit.
Race, class, denomination and doctrine separate the people of God.
Sunday morning is the most segregated time of the week. There are
over thirty thousand recognized Protestant denominations, and
many of them reject every other denomination but their own.

> Do you agree that
> Sunday morning is the
> most segregated time of
> the week? Why or why
> not?

Why? Because we have adopted a
false narrative that gives us permission to separate from those who are
different from us in appearance or
status or belief. It goes something like this: "If you do not look like us,
act like us, worship like us or think like us, we are not obligated to
have fellowship with you."

Anglos worship with Anglos; Hispanics worship with Hispanics.
Wealthy people attend church with wealthy people; poor people attend church with poor people. People who believe the Bible is inerrant fellowship only with those who believe the same; people who
believe homosexuality is an acceptable lifestyle fellowship only with

those who affirm same-sex relationships.

I once attended a talk where the speaker sprinkled salt and pepper on a metal sheet. He then shook it, and the pepper and the salt began to separate. He then went on to say that the races, like the salt and pepper, will always naturally separate, that blacks want to be with blacks and whites with whites, and that his illustration proved this was natural and God-ordained. This speech was given in a church. It was a clear example of the false narrative and a rationale to support it. Of course, this had nothing to do with racial separation. Salt and pepper separate because of weight, not color. Nonetheless, I looked around and saw people nodding in agreement, as if they were saying, "Yes, people of the same race should not worship together." It was appalling.

Do you speak in tongues? Do you sing hymns or praise music? Do you believe women can be pastors? Do you allow instruments in your sanctuary? These are questions we use to find out what people believe and practice, and the answers determine whether we can worship together. Some even question the salvation of those who answer differently. The sad fact is this: our divisions simply cannot be the way Jesus intended it to be. The false narrative of this chapter—if we disagree, then we must divide— allows this to happen and keeps it happening. Remember, we need a rationale for our behavior. Our actions are built on our ideas and narratives. Therefore, in order to overcome this problem, we need to replace the false narrative with the true narrative, the one found in the New Testament.

> What do you think about the notion that "if we disagree we must divide"? Do you consider this to be a false narrative?

THE FEAR BEHIND THE FALSE NARRATIVE

I do not believe that the church leaders who rejected me did so with malice toward me as much as fear. They were afraid that if they accepted my position they would be allowing something dangerous into their midst. Their position on *only two means of grace* has a long history, and they had concluded long ago that the inclusion of other means of grace diminished the sanctity of baptism and Communion, and overly elevated prayer and Bible reading. They were being protective in order to preserve the truth, which is probably why they were promoted to leadership. We want our shepherds to guard the flock.

Even when the motive is benign, we must not let our fears dictate our behavior. Perfect love casts out fear, because the kingdom is never in trouble. The gates of hell will not be shaken by correct doctrine but by the passionate hearts of men and women who have let go of their fears and moved forward in confidence that Christ is Lord and every knee will bow and every tongue confess it to be true. At the core of our fear is a desire to control. Exclusion allows us the feeling that we are safe; we have kept the false teachers out; we have cast out of the fellowship the wolves in sheep's clothing, and all is well. Insistence on doctrinal correctness is often a smoke screen that hides a deeper problem: our insecurity that all will crumble if we don't get everything right. The same is true for racial and gender differences. If people look or act different than we do, we become uncomfortable because we cannot fully understand them or control their behavior.

So, how do we overcome this in the body of Christ? Stanley Hauerwas explains: "This love that is characteristic of God's kingdom is possible only for a forgiven people—a people who have learned not to fear one another. . . . Only when my self—my character—has been formed by God's love, do I know I have no reason to fear the other."

Hauerwas pinpoints the problem: we fear each other. Much of that fear can be overcome by increasing our understanding of different races and cultures. But ultimately we overcome those fears by becoming people who know they are forgiven and are being formed by God's love.

The truth is that we will never get everything right. Who am I to say to another, "My doctrines, dogmas and definitions are perfect"? (Of course, I am addressing relationships within the church, not our relationship with those outside.) I see through a glass dimly when it comes to these minor matters. We simply must not divide over things we cannot fully understand. Especially in light of the fact that what we can understand, what is not a murky mystery but a blinding truth, is something we can all agree on: *Jesus is Lord!*

If your heart beats in love for Jesus, then take my hand and we will walk together in fellowship.

TRUE NARRATIVE:
CHRIST-FOLLOWERS MUST REMAIN UNIFIED

It is misguided to think that we Christians are always going to agree on every issue. It is also true that our cultural and worship practices differ. Accepting our differences is imperative, but they are no grounds for division. The true narrative, I believe, goes something like this: *If you do not look, act, worship or believe as I do, but your heart beats in love for Jesus, then regardless of our differences, we can and must have fellowship with one another.*

Many Christians have found a way to support the schism that is alarmingly prevalent in our day through the false narrative that disagreement allows for division. The true narrative, I believe, allows for disagreement, but not for division. We do not have to agree about style of worship or certain minor points of doctrine, but we can and must have fellowship if we hold to the central belief about Jesus. Which is why I can boldly proclaim: *Jesus is Lord!*

If your heart beats in love for Jesus, then take my hand and we will walk together in fellowship. He is Lord of those who insist that women cannot serve in ministry and Lord of those who insist they can. He is Lord of the Baptists and of the Episcopalians, Lord of those who speak in tongues and those who do not.

Styles of worship, dress codes, methods of baptism and differences of opinion about church polity simply cannot tear asunder what God has joined together. The church is a unified body, held together by Jesus. We may think we are divided, but we are not. I believe that all denominations that affirm the basic doctrines found in the creeds (i.e., the Apostles' Creed and the Nicene Creed) comprise the church in its many forms, whether they like it or not! I do not believe this because I am fond of unity and against diversity; I hold this position because I believe it is the teaching of Jesus and Paul.

JESUS' NARRATIVE: I PRAY THEY MAY BE ONE

Jesus knew that his disciples would come from all nations and races. In fact, he even commissioned his disciples to reach out to those outside of Judaism. In the Great Commission, Jesus instructed: "Go therefore and make disciples of all nations, baptizing them in the name of the Father and of the Son and of the Holy Spirit" (Matthew 28:19).

The Greek word for "nations" is *ethnos*, from which we get the word "ethnic." Jesus commands his disciples to go and make disciples of people from all ethnic backgrounds. Jesus unites all people, regardless of race, culture or creed, into one fellowship. Their unity is established in their baptism in the name of the Father, Son and Spirit. The many become one in the name of the Trinity.

Jesus knew that the invitation would be given not only to the Jews but also to those outside of Israel. He stated this clearly: "I have other sheep that do not belong to this fold. I must bring them also, and they will listen to my voice. So there will be one flock, one shepherd" (John 10:16). Gentiles would hear his voice and join the one flock under the leading of one Shepherd. The key word here is *one*. God's divine plan has always been to unite people of all nations into an all-inclusive community of loving persons who live under God's generous provision.

That is God's plan, and it does not include division. Just as the Trinity is unified, so the body of Christ is one. Jesus' famous prayer in John 17 illustrates this desire: "I ask not only on behalf of these, but also on behalf of those who will believe in me through their word, that they may all be one. As you, Father, are in me and I am in you, may they also be in us, so that the world may believe that you have sent me" (John 17:20-21).

Jesus is here anticipating the future when people would become his apprentices through the witness of his disciples. He is praying for unity within the *ecclesia*, the same kind of unity experienced in the mutual indwelling of the Father and the Son: "you are in me and I am in you." Jesus did not believe that our differences should divide us. Unity in the fellowship comes from a single source: Jesus.

PAUL'S NARRATIVE: WE ARE ONE IN CHRIST

For the first two decades after the resurrection and ascension of Jesus, Christians were primarily Jews who accepted Jesus as the Messiah. But thanks to the ministry of Paul, who had been commissioned to work as "an apostle to the Gentiles" (Romans 11:13), the gospel spread beyond Judaism. By the mid-50s A.D. churches from Jerusalem to Rome consisted of people from all different races and backgrounds. Despite their differences, they were *one*. Paul explained the ground for their unity:

> There is no longer Greek and Jew, circumcised and uncircumcised, barbarian, Scythian, slave and free; but Christ is all and in all! (Colossians 3:11)

> There is no longer Jew or Greek, there is no longer slave or free, there is no longer male and female; for all of you are one in Christ Jesus. (Galatians 3:28)

Paul is explaining the diversity and the unity of the *ecclesia* of Jesus. Jew and Greek, male and female, slave and master were one in Christ. Even the barbarian and the Scythian were welcome in the fellowship. Barbarians did not speak Greek and were thought to be uncivilized. Scythians were considered ruthless, crude and violent. Yet Paul included them in his list, showing that even those who seem to have no possibility for fellowship find their unity in Christ. Notice the phrase in Colossians 3:11: "Christ is all and in all." This is the central reason for our unity. Christ is in the female as well as the male, in the Jew as well as the Greek, even in the barbarian and the Scythian! Christ within is the bond of our unity. Though we differ on the outside, we are people indwelt by Christ, and therefore we, who differ in externals, become one because of who we are internally.

What might this have felt like to the members of the church in Colossae? Imagine you are Jewish, taught from birth that you are chosen by God and that the Gentiles are defiled, and having to join hands with a Greek for prayer. Or imagine you are a slaveholder, a member of the elite class, and reaching out to receive a piece of Communion bread from a slave. Imagine you are a first-century man raised with the notion that women are inferior, and looking across the room at a woman who, by her graciousness, has paid for the home you are meeting in. The cross-centered community discovered a kind of equality unknown in the first century.

If you were making this list to reflect contemporary churches, who would you include in your categories?

ONE CUP, ONE LOAF, ONE BODY

The act of Communion, also called the Lord's Supper or the Eucharist, has been a cause for division through the centuries. Even Reformers like Luther, Calvin and Zwingli argued a great deal about the meaning of Communion. Today there are just as many if not more divisions over its nature and practice. This is ironic, given that one of Paul's favorite metaphors to describe the unity of the fellowship was the Lord's Supper: "The cup of blessing that we bless, is it not a sharing in the blood of Christ? The bread that we break, is it not a sharing in the body of Christ? Because there is one bread, *we who are many are one body,* for we all partake of the one bread" (1 Corinthians 10:16-17, italics added).

Communion is a visible demonstration of how we who are many become one by uniting in the body and blood of Jesus. At the church where my family worships, I am frequently asked to help serve Communion. One Sunday, several years ago, I was struck by something I had never noticed before: people's hands.

Usually I distribute the bread (or wafer) by handing it to people, who hold out their hands to receive it. On this particular Sunday I was struck by how everyone's hands looked different: some were small, some large; some were calloused, some soft; some were wrinkled, some smooth; some had deformities, some were strong and healthy. All of these different hands were reaching out and receiving the same loaf. Their uniqueness and diversity found oneness and unity in the body of Christ. In fact, they were not only partaking of the body of Christ, they *were* the body of Christ.

We belong to one another. Our differences are not a hindrance but a welcome part of the body. The apostle wrote, "So we, who are many, are one body in Christ, and individually we are members one of another" (Romans 12:5).

On that day I remember feeling connected to the people in a way I had never experienced before. Those hands, those begging hands, reaching forward for the bread of heaven, became one in Christ. In several places Paul uses the metaphor of the body to describe how many become one. Hands and feet, eyes and ears, kneecaps and elbows are all different, yet find their unity in being a part of the same body.

AND ONE MIND

Apprentices of Jesus are united because they share the one cup, the one loaf, and are one body, but Paul takes it one step further by encouraging Christ-followers to be of *one mind:*

Finally, brothers, good-by. Aim for perfection, listen to my appeal, be of one mind, live in peace. And the God of love and peace will be with you. (2 Corinthians 13:11 NIV)

I appeal to you, brothers, in the name of our Lord Jesus Christ, that all of you agree with one another so that there may be no divisions among you and that you may be perfectly united in mind and thought. (1 Corinthians 1:10 NIV)

In both of these verses Paul appeals to the people to be united in their thinking. I suspect this is because he knows how easily people divide on the basis of race and class, and also on the basis of teaching, ideology or doctrine.

He pleads for them to "agree with one another so that there may be no divisions" among them. But this leads to the question: How can we agree with people who refuse to agree with us? How can we be "united in mind and thought" when clearly we do not agree on every point? Should we simply let go of our ideas, opinions or doctrines? We will never agree on all things, but we can and must agree on one thing: Jesus is Lord. The only way for us to "agree with one another," as Paul admonished the Corinthians, is to make the crucial distinction between essentials and nonessentials, and to find ways to love one another when our nonessentials differ. For an example of this, we can turn to an eighteenth-century man named John, who offered a helpful way for us to stay united even when we disagree.

IN ESSENTIALS UNITY, IN NONESSENTIALS CHARITY
Augustine is given credit for the quote "In essentials, unity; in doubtful matters, liberty; in all things, charity." If in fact it came from Augustine, it was his way of dealing with the difficult matter of disagreement in the church. It is a helpful principle that offers us a way to think about how we can stay unified even when we disagree. John Wesley liked this aphorism and modified it slightly in his preaching to the early Methodists.

The early Methodist societies consisted of people from different classes and backgrounds. Wesley quickly saw the problem of division on the basis of class, and he solved it (somewhat) by asking those who were wealthy not to dress in clothing that would set them apart from those who were poor. In the matter of division on the basis of doctrine, Wesley found a solution, as explained in his famous sermon "The Catholic Spirit" (the word *catholic* does not here refer to the Roman Catholic Church but rather means *universal*).

Wesley believed that the only way for the church to be unified was to learn how to distinguish between essentials and nonessentials, discover how to accept our differences in the nonessentials, and then decide not to let the differences overshadow our common faith. He believed love and commitment to Jesus were essential. Everything else was simply nonessential. He did not mean unimportant; he meant that those things should not divide us.

Wesley allowed differences of opinion, but he, like Paul, appealed to the Methodists not to let their differences prevent them from loving each other. In two sections of "The Catholic Spirit" Wesley states the matter clearly: "But although a difference of opinions or modes of worship may prevent an entire external union, yet need it prevent our union in affection? Though we can't think alike, may we not love alike? May we not be of one heart, though we are not of one opinion? Without all doubt we may."

Later in the sermon, Wesley gets more specific:

> I ask not therefore of him with whom I would unite in love, "Are you of my Church? Of my congregation?" . . . I inquire not, "Do you receive the Supper of the Lord in the same posture and manner that I do?" . . . Nay, I ask not of you . . . whether you allow baptism and the Lord's Supper at all. Let all these things stand by: we will talk of them, if need be, at a more convenient season. My only question at present is this, "Is thine heart right, as my heart is with thy heart?" (39.1.11)

We can, and will, differ in how we think, which style of worship we prefer, which method of baptism we affirm, but these are not essential. The only thing that matters is that our hearts beat in love for Jesus. If we have that, we are united. Then we can say once again: *Jesus is Lord!*

If your heart beats in love for Jesus, then take my hand and we will walk together in fellowship.

NOT UNIMPORTANT, JUST NOT IMPORTANT ENOUGH

I preached at a vibrant church in the Northeast and found myself impressed with everything about their life together. They loved one another, and they worshiped with enthusiasm. Children, youth, young adults, adults and the elderly all gathered together as one body. I was inspired by being with them. After the event I went to the pastor's office to gather up my things and to wait for the pastor to take me to the airport. I soon realized that an important meeting was going on, so I sat outside of his door in the waiting area. Though I did not intend to eavesdrop, the door was open, so I could hear what was going on. They spoke in hushed tones, so I knew it was a serious matter.

"We know we must leave the denomination," the pastor said, "because we disagree on a fundamental issue. And we know the church supports the separation—the vote was 92 percent in favor of separating and joining a new denomination. The only question is, who owns the building?"

"Right. That is the problem. Technically, our current denomination owns the property. If we split, we will have to move out," a man said. "Our lawyers think we can fight it in court, but we could lose and spend a lot of money trying. The general consensus is that we need to fight it, though. The people feel like it is *their* church. They paid for it, they built it, they were baptized here and married here, and they buried their loved ones here."

The meeting lasted for about fifteen minutes, and then they tabled the discussion for a later time. The pastor came out of his office and said, "Sorry, Jim. It was an urgent meeting. Are you ready to go to the airport?" I told him I was. While driving on the freeway I could tell he was still deep in thought about the meeting he had just had. He asked, "Did you overhear our discussion?"

"Yes," I said. "I was not trying to . . ."

"No, I am glad you did. I was wondering what you think. Do you think we should fight to keep our building?" he asked.

"Do you really want to know what I think? You may not like it," I said.

"Please tell me. I won't be offended."

"Well, I don't think you should fight it," I said. "In fact, I don't think you should split from the denomination."

"Jim, are you serious? How can we stay? The church has gotten too liberal. We can't stay tied to a group that believes what they affirm," he said with a little anger in his voice.

"Has the denomination denied the deity of Jesus, the reality of the resurrection or the triune God?" I asked.

"No. But they are affirming principles that are not backed by the Bible. In fact, they are denying the authority of the Bible."

"Have they made that statement: 'We reject the authority of the Bible'?" I asked.

"No. But by holding their position—which is against the Bible's teaching—they are in fact rejecting it."

"Rejecting the Bible or rejecting your understanding of what the Bible teaches?" I asked again.

"Jim, I thought you were a conservative Christian. You preach about Jesus, and you preach from the Bible."

"I am not a liberal or a conservative. I am an apprentice of Jesus. I am simply trying to discern that which is essential and that which is nonessential. For me, the basic teaching found in the creeds

> What difference is there between rejecting the Bible and rejecting a particular interpretation in the Bible?

is essential. Everything else is nonessential. Not unimportant, just not important enough for me to divide from those who share the same belief in the essentials. I actually agree with your church's position on this issue, but I would not divide over it, because it is a nonessential to me."

"Well, that is a fair point. I guess I and the majority in our church believe that this issue *is* an essential," he said. "That is why we must split."

I told him I appreciated his heart and his desire to be faithful to God. I dearly love this pastor and his people. They made a choice to split, a choice I did not affirm but understood and accepted. I stand in unity with them. Though I disagree with their choice to split, they are my brothers and sisters in Christ, and in my eyes we are one. They still believe in the same essentials as I do, and that is our *unity*. We disagree over what I believe is a nonessential, and for that reason I offer them *charity*.

CHALLENGES TO UNITY IN THE CHURCH

Thus far I have focused mainly on the divisions in the church that come from disagreement about doctrine. I want to return to Paul's admonition in Colossians 3 to take a closer look at three other causes of separation in the church: race, gender and class. In the following verses Paul mentions these differences specifically:

> Here there is no Greek or Jew, circumcised or uncircumcised, barbarian, Scythian, slave or free, but Christ is all, and is in all. (Colossians 3:11 NIV)

> There is no longer Jew or Greek, there is no longer slave or free, there is no longer male and female; for all of you are one in Christ Jesus. (Galatians 3:28)

Notice the word *here* in Colossians 3:11. Where is the "here"? It is in the church. The *ecclesia* is a peculiar community rooted in another world—the kingdom of heaven. When the community gathers in the name of Jesus, they step out of this world and its natural divisions, and they become a united people.

How are we united? Both verses are clear: in Christ. Christ is in everyone, changing our fundamental identity. We are people in whom Christ dwells. This fact does not eradicate our differences. Men are still men and women are still women; the body of Christ does not comprise an androgynous people. Those who are Greek and those who are Jews remain Greeks and Jews by ethnicity. And those who were slaves are still slaves when they step outside of the community. Paul is saying that here, in the gathered community, we are one in Christ.

The solution to gender, race and social divisions is not to eradicate our differences but to see them in light of Jesus. The Pentecostal movement in the United States in the early twentieth century was astonishingly diverse. Blacks, whites and Latinos worshiped together, and women played an important role in ministry.

> When have you experienced a sense of unity with a diverse group of Christians? What created that unity?

They were fond of saying that the "color line was washed away in the blood of Jesus." This was because they saw their unity in the Spirit. Males and females, whites and blacks, rich and poor—all were conduits for the same Spirit. Equality was discovered not by disregarding differences but by finding the source of unity within their diversity.

The true source of our "unity in diversity" is the Trinity. The Trinity is neither black nor white nor male nor female; the divine persons are distinct and yet unified. Serene Jones writes, "God's very reality is radically multiple, radically relational, and infinitely active." The Father is distinct from the Son and the Spirit, and finds his identity in that difference. And yet, Father, Son and Spirit are one, mutually indwelling and mutually interdependent. That is why the church is both distinct and unified. The good and beautiful community is a mirror of the Trinity.

Distinctions in gender and race are not to be downplayed but affirmed as a part of God's beautiful creation. Outside of the church these distinctions cause suspicion and division, and are barriers to community; inside the church they can be celebrated and affirmed. N. T. Wright observes:

> These distinctions . . . have become irrelevant in Christ. . . . These barriers and habits are . . . neither natural or normal. They are, ultimately, a denial of the creation of humankind in the image of God. . . . [D]ifferences of background, nationality, colour, language, social standing and so forth must be regarded as irrelevant to the question of love, honor and respect that are to be shown to individuals and groups.

I would disagree slightly with the word *irrelevant* because our distinctions remain and are a part of the beauty of the body of Christ. While not irrelevant, race, gender and class, to use Wesley's phrase, are nonessentials when it comes to unity. The essential is our identity as people in whom Christ dwells. But Wright shifts the issue to the right place: these differences are indeed irrelevant to the question of love. Tolerance is not our primary aim, nor is equality; our highest aim is love. Our primary focus is on Christ as Lord. So we say, *Jesus is Lord!*

If your heart beats in love for Jesus, then take my hand and we will walk together in fellowship.

RICHARD'S DREAM

Richard J. Foster wrote one of the most important books on spiritual formation in the past hundred years, *Celebration of Discipline.* Not long after its initial success, Richard was troubled by something: individuals, not groups, were using the book in isolation, with the aim of personal spiritual growth. Richard believed that the disciplines—

with their roots in the ancient church—were not meant to separate but to unite. Under the leading of the Spirit he chose to take an eighteen-month sabbatical from writing and speaking. During that time he listened to God, and a clear message was given to him: the walls that separate our churches must come down.

In a vision like the dream given to Martin Luther King Jr., Foster was filled with a new hope for the church. He articulated it this way:

> Right now we largely remain a scattered people. This has been the condition of the Church of Jesus Christ for a good many years. But a new thing is coming. God *is* gathering his people once again, creating of them an all-inclusive community of loving persons with Jesus Christ as the community's prime sustainer and most glorious inhabitant. . . . I see a people . . . even though it feels as if I am peering through a glass darkly.
>
> I see a country pastor from Indiana embracing an urban priest from New Jersey and together praying for the peace of the world. I see a people.
>
> I see a Catholic monk from the hills of Kentucky standing alongside a Baptist evangelical from the streets of Los Angeles and together offering up a sacrifice of praise. I see a people.
>
> I see social activists from the urban centers of Hong Kong joining with Pentecostal preachers from the barrios of São Paulo and together weeping over the spiritually lost and the plight of the poor. I see a people.
>
> I see laborers from Soweto and landowners from Pretoria honoring and serving each other out of reverence for Christ. I see a people.
>
> I see Hutu and Tutsi, Serb and Croat, Mongol and Han Chinese, African-American and Anglo, Latino and Native American all sharing and caring and loving one another. I see a people.
>
> I see the sophisticated standing with the simple, the elite

standing with the dispossessed, the wealthy standing with the poor. I see a people.

This vision gave birth to Renovaré, a spiritual renewal ministry for churches that Richard and others established in 1988. Great strides have occurred through this ministry and others like it. The vision is strong and powerful because, I believe, it is the vision of God for his people.

CAN YOU OFFER CHARITY TO ME?

I suspect that this chapter will have challenged or even offended many readers. I have taken a bold position: we must view all who call on Jesus as our brothers and sisters regardless of doctrine or race or practice. I am aware that some of what I call nonessential will be, for others, essentials worth fighting for. I respect your position, and I pray you respect mine. I am still searching, still trying to follow the leading of the Spirit. I pray that you extend to me the same charity that I offer you, the charity to love and accept you as a member of Christ's body, as someone who is important to me, even if we disagree. I know we agree on one thing, and it is my hope that it is strong enough to hold us all together: *Jesus is Lord!*

If your heart beats in love for Jesus, then take my hand and we will walk together in fellowship.

LOVING THOSE WE DISAGREE WITH

John Wesley not only gave us a helpful way to stay unified even if we disagree, but also in that same sermon he offered five ways we can show love to those with whom we differ or disagree in the non-essentials:

1. Treat them as companions.
2. Do not think or speak evil of them.
3. Pray for them.
4. Encourage them to do good.
5. Collaborate with them in ministry.

These excellent suggestions will go a long way toward helping us not only to get along but also to love fellow Christians we have differences with.

This week, think about a church or a friend or fellow Christian who belongs to a church other than yours. It may be that you know someone or a local church whose doctrines and practices are different than yours. See if you can implement some or all of Wesley's ideas. What might this look like?

Treat them as companions. Ask the person to lunch. If it is a church you are feeling led to connect with in this way, worship with them.

Do not speak or think evil of them. Be sure to refrain from pointing out your differences, either to the person or to others. Focus on what you have in common.

Pray for them. Make that person or that church the special object of your prayers this week.

Encourage them to do good. During lunch or worship, or whenever you connect, be sure to encourage the person in the good work he or she is already doing. Ask questions and find out what the person, or the church, is doing in ministry, and be affirming.

Collaborate with them. If at all possible, see if you can work alongside the person (or church), either in something he or she is doing, or in some ministry in which you are engaged. Working alongside someone creates a bond of unity that overcomes our differences.

OTHER EXERCISES

In addition, find time this week to pray not only for those who differ but for the body of Christ and its leaders. The following are two ways we can do this:

1. Pray for the unity of the church. As you pray for the unity of the church you will find yourself shifting the focus from how we differ in ideas or practices, and onto the One who holds us all together.

2. Pray for pastors and leaders. If the church is to unite in new ways, it will likely come from the leaders. Pray for pastors and other church leaders to catch the same vision that captured the mind of Richard Foster. If you want, use Richard's vision as a guide for your prayers.

five

The Reconciling Community

Stan is a former student of mine who taught me a great deal about forgiveness and reconciliation. He was a tall, handsome, athletic, shy young man. He sat in the back of the class, never spoke and seldom made eye contact. One day he came to my office unannounced, and when he sat down I could see he was shaking. He put his head in his hands and did not speak for five minutes; he just sobbed, and I waited. Finally he told me that he needed help. The night before, he said, he had attempted suicide; then he noted, "But just like in everything I do, I failed." I told him I was glad he failed. He took a long look at me, the first real eye contact he ever made with me. He was looking to see if he was safe. "You can tell me whatever you want, Stan," I said gently.

"I was sexually abused for the past five years, starting when I was thirteen. The man who took advantage of me is an old friend of our family. He was like an uncle to me—taking me camping, teaching me how to play sports. I trusted him. Then the abuse started. He told me that if I ever told anyone, bad things would happen to me, and then people would know how bad I am. You are the first person I have ever told." He looked at me again, to see if I was judging him.

"So you feel trapped. Is that why you attempted suicide?" I asked.

"Yes. I thought it was the only way out. Later last night I remembered some things you said in class about God and about hope. That is why I wanted to talk with you," said Stan.

We proceeded to talk for about an hour. I sensed that Stan needed to speak with a professional counselor, and fortunately we offer that service free on our campus. I set up an appointment for him, and he went twice a week for the next month. I saw him on campus, and he waved to me. He did not look well, but he was managing. The next time I saw him was in chapel, on a day when I was preaching about God's acceptance and forgiveness. Stan followed me to my office and asked to talk. We sat down with coffee.

"Is that true?" he asked.

"Is what true?"

"What you said in chapel—about God's unconditional love and forgiveness?"

"I believe every word I said, Stan."

"So how do you do it?" he asked.

"Do you mean, how do you experience that?"

"Yeah," he said. "I went to church some growing up, but I never heard that message. All I remember hearing was that we are supposed to try harder so that we won't go to hell."

"God doesn't want you to try any harder, Stan, he just wants to love you, and for you to love him back. When you love God with your whole heart, the rest takes care of itself."

"I really want to know that love," he said, as if his soul were starving.

"Let's pray," I said.

I prayed that God would reveal himself to Stan, to come into his heart. Stan whispered, "Yes, God, please come into my heart." The prayer lasted only five minutes, but when we sat up and our eyes met I noticed that his countenance had changed. He was beaming with joy.

"What do I do now?" he asked.

"Do you have a Bible?"

"No."

"Do you have a group of Christian friends to meet with?"

"No."

"Then I will take care of both. Keep Thursday night free."

He said he would. I called two students who were active in their faith and asked them to get to know Stan. I told them that I was going to get him a Bible. They asked if they could do it. I said sure. They pooled their money and bought Stan his first Bible. That Thursday night he showed up early and sat in front with his new Bible and a notepad. He wrote down everything I said, and was flipping through his Bible, trying to read every passage I referenced. I had been teaching on how we are new creations in Christ. The metaphor I used was the transformation of a caterpillar into a butterfly. Stan was smiling; he liked that image. Afterward, his two new friends took him out for coffee and talked with him late into the night.

He told them his story, and the other students did not judge him but told him that they loved him. He had found friends. He never missed our Thursday-night fellowship group. About a month after asking God into his heart, Stan stopped by my office. He said, "If it would be all right with you, I would like to share my testimony at the campus fellowship." He had only been with us a month and he already knew our lingo: "share my testimony"! I told him he could. The next week I introduced him and said, "Stan wants to share his own story about discovering God's love." He got up and stammered for a moment, but then launched into his own story. He held nothing back. He was completely transparent, telling them about his abuse, his self-hatred and his suicide attempt.

Then his countenance changed, just as it did in my office, when he began talking about how God reached out and came into his heart, about the warm feeling of acceptance and forgiveness he felt, and how his life was changed. "I have one last thing to say," he said and then paused. "I was once a caterpillar. But Christ Jesus lives in me. And I am now a butterfly!" There was not a dry eye in the room. Stan sat down, and I walked to the center of the room. I did not feel like teaching after that. It turned out I would not need to. A young woman raised her hand and then stood up and said, "I was also abused when I was young. It went on for a year. I have carried that burden for a long time, but Stan's courage has inspired me. Tonight I want to let the pain out." We prayed for her, asking God to loosen and release the pain.

Stan had one more thing to teach me. He came to my office a few months later and said, "I have a question. Since God forgave me of all of my sins, then I figure that he would also forgive the man who molested me. I want to tell him about Jesus, and that I forgive him for what he did to me. Do you think that is a good idea?" he asked.

I was stunned. Here he was, ready to forgive the person who had nearly caused the end of his life, a man who for five years had torn his soul apart. Everything in me wanted to say, "No, you must not forgive him!" I realized that my own heart was far from forgiving this man, whom I had never even met. I paused and prayed, then said, "If you feel led to forgive him, then I would not forbid it. But please be careful. He will likely not listen to you. To forgive someone implies their guilt, and he may be in denial."

"I am prepared. I want him to know what I know. Maybe he could turn his life around if he knew about God's love and forgiveness," Stan said. I was right, however, about the man being in denial. He acted as if nothing had happened, and he said he didn't want to hear

> In our soul-training exercises, we encounter the idea that "hurt people hurt people." Stan extends forgiveness in the way that we receive forgiveness. Is there someone that you could extend forgiveness to?

about God. But Stan did one thing that surprised me. He said to the man as they were parting, "I forgive you. But I want you to know one thing: you will never take advantage of me again. I am not afraid anymore. I am a butterfly."

FALSE NARRATIVE: ONLY WHEN WE FORGIVE WILL WE BE FORGIVEN AND HEALED

I have had the privilege of being a guest on many Christian radio talk shows. Typically, the host of the show interviews me about the content or ideas from one of my books. Many of the shows allow listeners to call in and ask questions. Initially, I expected callers to join in the discussion, perhaps agreeing or disagreeing with me or raising a question about the topic. However, I quickly learned that seldom happens. Instead, listeners often share their stories that end with the same plea: "I have been hurt by someone—please help me forgive them."

Often it concerns some form of betrayal, usually between spouses: a husband left his wife for another woman or vice versa. Sometimes people want to find the courage to forgive themselves for having made so many mistakes. One woman, barely holding back her tears, told of the years of bad decisions and drug abuse, and said she was at a place where she refused to forgive herself for destroying her own life: "I have made so many mistakes I cannot forgive myself." One time a man said, with trembling voice, "My wife up and left me and our kids. I do not know where she is, but I still love her, and would take her back if she asked. Is that right? If she walked through our door right now, I would forgive her, I think. Do you think I should?"

No matter what the topic of the program was supposed to be, I could count on at least two of the calls being about forgiveness: Can I forgive? Should I forgive? How do I forgive? These real-life stories and questions always made me pause and reflect on two powerful points: First, people want to be free of the pain that has been inflicted by another person (which they assume forgiveness will cure).

Second, it is very hard to forgive people who have hurt us.

One day, while in my car, I was listening to a therapist who has a radio call-in show. Sure enough, he got a call from a desperate person who asked, "How can I forgive a person who has hurt me?" I eagerly turned up the volume to hear his answer.

"Well, let me make this clear. Forgiveness is something you do for you. You need to forgive this person in order to be healed. Your pain will not go away until you forgive that person," the therapist said with authority.

Then it hit me—you cannot forgive by power of the will. This therapist was wrong. The false narrative that hurts so many people goes like this: Only when we forgive will we be forgiven and healed. This false narrative tells us that *forgiveness is something we must do* because God commanded it, or because we are tired of the pain unforgiveness is causing us. The false narrative that we must do the work of forgiving is yet another version of the control narratives we so easily adopt because they seem to make sense to us, and because they allow us the illusion that we can control everything. If forgiveness is something I do out of my own strength, then I get the credit if I succeed or the blame if I fail. So we grit our teeth and try to feel forgiveness toward someone who has harmed us. And we fail.

> What do you think of the idea that the false narrative ultimately centers around the idea that we must choose to forgive?

We fail because *we do not have the resources to forgive.* On our own, in our weak flesh, we do not have the strength or capacity to forgive the trespasses of those who trespass against us, no matter how hard we try. The only way we can forgive is by letting God renarrate our lives in the context of the metanarrative of Jesus, who forgave his enemies and even died for them. This will lead to healing—the healing of ourselves—which is necessary if we are going to forgive someone who has hurt us.

TRUE NARRATIVE: KNOWING WE HAVE BEEN FORGIVEN LEADS TO HEALING AND FORGIVENESS

Stan taught me what the New Testament teaches but somehow I had failed to understand. Stan's life, his story, became a part of the metanarrative of Jesus, and he was able to renarrate his story in light of the story of the cross—the solid fact that God in Christ has reconciled the world to himself. With all due respect to those who counsel from a secular perspective (and do a great deal of good for people), in Stan's case the counselor he saw was merely able to help him become stabilized, not to be healed, and certainly not to transform his pain into joy. For that he needed to graft his life into a story that helped him see what had happened to him in a new light.

> Forgiveness does not mean subjecting yourself to continued victimization. When have you felt the need for good boundaries?

As is common in people who have been abused, Stan blamed himself. He could not forgive himself, he told me, because what he had done was so evil, even if he was not complicit. It was only when Stan saw his life, his story, as a part of God's story that he was able to confront his memories and his abuser with the ability to forgive. Jesus had borne his sins—all of them—on the cross and announced, "It is finished." Christ had forgiven him, and now he was empowered to forgive. It would not take a lot of willpower on his part to forgive; it was a natural extension of grace. The true narrative is this: Only when we know we have been forgiven will we find healing and become able to forgive.

Stan asked me, the morning of his conversion, if what I was preaching was true. What I was preaching, to be more specific, was based on this passage from 2 Corinthians: "All this is from God, who reconciled us to himself through Christ, and has given us the ministry of reconciliation; that is, in Christ God was reconciling the world to himself, not counting their trespasses against them, and entrusting the message of reconciliation to us" (2 Corinthians 5:18-19).

This is a clear explanation of the finality of the cross. God—in Christ—is not counting our sins against us. God stopped counting and apparently never took it back up. God is no longer dealing with us on the basis of our sins but of our faith. Jesus died for all of the sins of all of the people for all time—and that means you. Do you know that? Do you have that peace that passes all understanding? Do you have the joy of knowing that God has nothing against you? When Stan walked into the chapel that day, he would have answered these questions with a no. When he left my office, thanks to the powerful work of the Holy Spirit, he could say yes.

For years, the transformation I saw in Stan had always been a sacred miracle to me, something I was privileged to witness but did not understand. Only years later, when I understood the transforming power of narrative, spiritual exercise and community, did I find ways of understanding what happened to him. Stan renarrated his story in the larger context of God's story, and he did it in the context of community. He then began unlearning destructive patterns and instead began practicing forgiveness and reconciliation. But note: he did not have to try. Healing was happening to him. When he knew that Jesus had forgiven him, he began to forgive himself. Knowing he had been forgiven began a process of healing.

Stan did not forgive in order to feel better, though his pain had driven him to the end of his rope. He was already feeling better before he forgave the man. He was feeling better because his heart had been warmed by the good news that sins, *even his*, had been forgiven. It was not for his own therapy that Stan addressed his abuser, but a natural extension of the grace he had found—or that had found him. We can only forgive when we know we have been forgiven, when we are certain that we live in the strong and safe kingdom of God.

JESUS' NARRATIVE

What is the narrative of Jesus concerning forgiveness and reconciliation?

Jesus told his apprentices a story to illustrate this concept of forgiving others because we have been forgiven. He did so, however, in reverse: the story he told is about a person who has been forgiven much but fails to forgive even a little. In this story Jesus used money, or debt, as a metaphor for forgiveness in general:

> For this reason the kingdom of heaven may be compared to a king who wished to settle accounts with his slaves. When he began the reckoning, one who owed him ten thousand talents was brought to him; and, as he could not pay, his lord ordered him to be sold, together with his wife and children and all his possessions, and payment to be made. So the slave fell on his knees before him, saying, "Have patience with me, and I will pay you everything." And out of pity for him, the lord of that slave released him and forgave him the debt. (Matthew 18:23-27)

In this parable a king is settling his accounts, and comes across a man who owes him an outrageous amount of money: ten thousand talents. The debtor cannot pay this huge debt and begs the king for mercy. Amazingly, the king cancels the man's debt, and he walks away free. He and his whole family could have spent the rest of their lives as slaves in a distant land or in debtors' prison. Thanks to the mercy of the king, he lives in freedom.

You would think that anyone who had been forgiven a debt so great would be the most gracious, merciful and generous person on the planet. Yet this was not the case.

> But that same slave, as he went out, came upon one of his fellow slaves who owed him a hundred denarii; and seizing him by the throat, he said, "Pay what you owe." Then his fellow slave fell down and pleaded with him, "Have patience with me, and I will

pay you." But he refused; then he went and threw him into prison until he would pay the debt. (Matthew 18:28-30)

The man who had been forgiven so much bumps into a man who owes him, in comparison, very little, a hundred denarii (about a couple months' salary). The shock of the story is the difference in the amount of the debt. Ten thousand talents is approximately *six hundred thousand times more* than one hundred denarii. Even though he had been released from an enormous amount of money, the man who should be forgiving has his debtor thrown into prison!

When the king hears of this, he brings the unforgiving man back into his presence to confront him about this inequity, saying: "'You wicked slave! I forgave you all that debt because you pleaded with me. Should you not have had mercy on your fellow slave, as I had mercy on you?' And in anger his lord handed him over to be tortured until he would pay his entire debt" (Matthew 18:32-34). The king has the unforgiving man thrown in prison to work off his debt, which he will never be able to repay.

What is the point of the parable? Keep in mind the question this story was designed to answer: how much and how often should we forgive one another? The king is like God, and we are like the man who owes the king a debt we cannot pay. We can never hope to earn God's forgiveness. Our sins are too great and we simply have nothing we could offer God to repay them. However, the king forgives the unrepayable debt out of mercy, just as God, in Christ, has forgiven our unrepayable debt. The man did nothing to merit his forgiven debt, and neither do we. The point is clear: we have been forgiven for so much more than we will ever be called on to forgive.

Journal on the idea of imbalance in the forgiveness we receive compared to the forgiveness we offer.

Let me be clear, lest you think I am encouraging the false narrative, insinuating that you simply must forgive out of your own strength or will. Jesus told this story in order to help us get our narratives right. If we meditate for a long time on how much we have been forgiven, it will help us forgive others. Stan understood this without reading this passage. He said, "Since God forgave me of all of my sins, then I figure that he would also forgive the man who molested me. I want to tell him about Jesus, and that I forgive him for what he did to me."

Stan's narrative shifted dramatically in a relatively short period of time as he renarrated his own story: God has forgiven me for all of my sins, therefore, I can forgive those who have sinned against me. But note: it was only when the larger narrative was well in place that he was able to do it. If, on the day he told me about his years of molestation, I had said, "Stan, you need to forgive that man, and forgive yourself while you are at it," I would have done him much harm. He would have been thrown back on himself (the false narrative) and unable to forgive either that man or himself.

FORGIVEN ONLY WHEN WE FORGIVE?

Jesus' story ended with the unforgiving man being thrown into prison and tortured for the rest of his life. Then Jesus said to his disciples: "So my heavenly Father will also do to every one of you, if you do not forgive your brother or sister from your heart" (Matthew 18:35).

It is easy to make a mistake here and assume that our forgiveness is conditioned on our ability to forgive, or that forgiveness is like a transaction: you forgive, then God will forgive you. Many people pray the Lord's Prayer ("Forgive us our trespasses as we forgive those who trespass against us") and conclude that our forgiveness is merited by our ability to forgive.

> Pause a moment to reflect on Volf's remark that Jesus forgives *through* us. How does this affect your interaction with the world around you?

This is yet another false narrative, and it is so deeply embedded in people that we need to take a moment to address it. Jesus is simply trying to show us the absurdity of accepting God's forgiveness for our countless sins and yet refusing to forgive the one or two (or even a hundred) sins done against us. It is absurd for us to glory in the forgiveness God has given us and yet remain unwilling to forgive someone who has harmed us.

A community who has been forgiven must become a community who forgives. God's forgiveness toward us is unrestricted; how can our forgiveness for one another be restricted? That is his point. Turning the story into a transaction reveals the tendency we have toward legalism. My inability to forgive another is usually based on my own sense of justice. We think, *It is unfair, unjust, to forgive the person who hurt me.* Why? They have not earned our forgiveness. True. So then, is that how we want to be treated? Jesus is saying to us, "All right, if it is your just deserts you are after, then you can have them. If it is justice you seek, it is justice you shall get." New Testament scholar Joachim Jeremias states it this way: "Woe unto you if you try to stand on your rights; God will then stand on his and see that his sentence is executed rigorously."

So which way do we want to be treated? By mercy or by justice? Dare we have the audacity to look to God and ask for our rights when it comes to those who have sinned against us, but ask for mercy when it comes to our own trespasses? We cannot play it both ways.

Jesus' words in the Lord's Prayer are reminders that we need to hear repeatedly: You have been forgiven much; therefore you must forgive. It is not easy, but it is also not impossible. Once we stand firmly entrenched in the larger story of our own forgiveness, we can then forgive—a process that often takes time. Not surprisingly, this is exactly what Paul taught in his epistles.

PAUL'S VIEW

In two places Paul exhorts the *ecclesia* to bear with each other and forgive each other, and in both places he does so on the basis that we have been forgiven by God:

> Bear with one another and, if anyone has a complaint against another, forgive each other; just as the Lord has forgiven you, so you also must forgive. (Colossians 3:13)

> Be kind to one another, tenderhearted, forgiving one another, as God in Christ has forgiven you. (Ephesians 4:32)

From these two passages I see both the *pattern* and the *power* of forgiveness. Paul is not suggesting we forgive. He is commanding us to "bear with one another" and to "be kind to one another." How is that done? By forgiving. As Christ forgave us, so we also forgive. It is not something we do—it is something we participate in. That is the pattern of forgiveness. L. Gregory Jones is helpful here: "The pattern of our forgiven-ness, and hence our discipleship as forgiven and forgiving people, is none other than the pattern we find in Christ."

It is unthinkable, then, for us to willfully not forgive those who have harmed us, because we have been forgiven. N. T. Wright explains: "Paul here makes two points. . . . First, it is utterly inappropriate for one who knows the joy and release of being forgiven to refuse to share that blessing with another. Second, it is highly presumptuous to refuse to forgive one whom Christ himself has already forgiven."

But before we turn this into an enterprise of the flesh, we must realize that we do not do this on our own. Our ability to forgive is not only patterned after Christ but empowered by Christ. As Miroslav Volf says so well, "Christ forgives through us, and that is why we can forgive." Jesus then is both the *pattern* and the *power* of forgiveness and reconciliation.

WE ALL NEED FORGIVENESS

When I was just out of seminary and serving my first years in the local church, I had the privilege of meeting on a regular basis my former professor and mentor Richard J. Foster. By this time Richard was a highly respected and famous speaker and writer on the Christian life. Richard suggested that we get together once a week to share with one another about our lives and pray. I always showed up with great enthusiasm. Each week he taught me something new.

One of the things he taught me has especially stuck with me through the years. For a few weeks I was struggling in my life with God because of my proneness to wander from the God I love. I really wanted to unburden myself, to break the power of this pattern, and I knew in my heart that I needed to confess it to someone and bring it to the light. I also wanted Richard to think well of me, so I ruled him out as the person I would confess to. Then, during our next meeting, he said, "Jim, is there anything you would like to confess?" I was shocked and wondered how he could have possibly known. I stammered, "Well, yes, there is. I want to confess—" but he cut me off. He then said, "I will be happy to hear your confession and announce God's forgiveness over you, but first you must hear my confession." I was stunned. The great and spiritual Richard Foster could sin? And even more shocking was that he would confess it to me. I was not worthy. For a few moments I was disoriented. Then, rather sheepishly, I said, "Okay."

Richard then proceeded to confess his own sins of that past week. Years later I am certain that he confessed not so much because he needed to but in order to teach me several things. First, all of us are sinners. I think he knew I put him on a pedestal, and he wanted me to know that we are all human. Second, he wanted to take away my fear. He could see I was hesitant to confess, so he, in a Christlike way, showed me the way. Third, he wanted to draw us closer. By disclosing our hearts in this way, we moved to a new level of trust. I believe that morning time of confession allowed us to trust one another in a new way.

KEEPING BOUNDARIES OF FORGIVENESS

This discussion would not be complete if I did not mention two caveats about forgiveness and reconciliation. The first deals with keeping appropriate boundaries. In the real world there is a great deal of pain, violence and tragedy, and people cannot be counted on to respond to our kindness with graciousness and integrity. Though we are called to love by forgiving, we need to be careful when and how we do this. Though we are called to be reconciled, we are not called to be abused or to be repeatedly harmed by someone. Though we are called to bear one another's burdens, we must remove ourselves from persons or situations that take advantage of us or can hurt us. To forgive is not to be abused.

There was a young man in a youth group I once led whose birth mother had abandoned him when he was three. He had been raised by his grandparents while his mother continued to spend her time abusing drugs and subsequently losing jobs. Once a year, as if on cue, she would reappear in this young man's life and try to reestablish their relationship. For a few weeks she would be around and would tell him she was sorry for the things she had done to him (such as locking him in a basement for two days) and not done for him (be a parent). He would find himself torn: he wanted to forgive her, but he also knew she would let him down.

I explained to him, "What you really want is to be loved by her, but she is not capable of that right now, and perhaps not for a long time, perhaps never. You can forgive her for what she has done to you, but you are old enough now to stop it from continuing. You need to set boundaries with her, as strange as that sounds. You can tell her you love her, and that you forgive her, but you must also tell her you will not let her keep hurting you." This made a great deal of sense to him, and he was able to set up appropriate boundaries with her. Many years have passed since those days. The last time I spoke with him, he told me that she had never changed her ways, but he also had never let her take advantage of him again. Now grown, married and a father himself, he told me he learned how to forgive without being abused.

THE FORGIVENESS AMBUSH

A second caveat or warning about forgiveness and reconciliation involves times when our need to feel forgiven disregards the possible hurt it may cause the person we are forgiving or asking for forgiveness. A colleague of mine was once involved in a chaplaincy program in which he worked closely with a group of a dozen or so pastors. In one of their meetings, a fellow pastor told the group she had something important to confess. She got up, walked over to my colleague, knelt down in front of him, and said she needed to ask for forgiveness for harboring anger and other ill feelings toward him—which she then listed in front of the group. My colleague said that he was extremely embarrassed and felt ashamed throughout the whole event. He had never known of her strong negative feelings, and now he would forever. And so would the rest of the group.

This kind of request for forgiveness does not build community—this is narcissism. And sometimes it is malicious, a way to attack someone under the guise of reconciliation. The pastor should have made her confession privately. And even then there is a danger that it is still more about her need to unload some emotional baggage than it is about strengthening a relationship. My friend Andrew calls this "the forgiveness ambush." A person calls you up for coffee and midway through your latte announces that he or she has something they feel led to discuss. Once again, it is all about that person's hurt or pain that you, unknowingly, have caused. "But I want you to know that I have forgiven you," the person often says. This is not genuine reconciliation. This is just showy forgiveness, making light of the true act of reconciliation.

If we truly have forgiven someone, we will not need to alert him or her to it. If it is a case of wanting to make the person aware of something that you feel he or she needs to change, that is entirely different. That is not reconciliation but admonishment (see chapter six). If one person truly has forgiven another, he or she would be better off showing it by taking the other person out for coffee and deepening the friendship through healthy conversation and perhaps a time of prayer together. If you have come to that blessed place where you have forgiven someone, keep it between you and God. Love, it is said, covers a multitude of sins (1 Peter 4:8).

A POWER MADE PERFECT IN WEAKNESS

For the first few years after he graduated, I had little contact with Stan. But eventually he did his best to reconnect with me and would call me once a year or so. After college he joined the Navy, becoming a part of the elite Navy Seals. He told me a few years later that he had gotten married, and the next year he told me about the birth of their first child.

He also told me that God has used him in a ministry to help young people who had been sexually abused. He shared his testimony on a regular basis with young people who were trying to put their lives together. I asked him what he tells them, and he said, "Oh, I just tell them my story. I tell them how I became a butterfly and that they can do the same." As I have grown more in my understanding, I see more clearly how Jesus stepped in and transformed a human life in only a few months. Jesus wrote Stan into his story, and Stan was never the same.

God has given us all a message of reconciliation—that God, in Christ, has reconciled the world to himself (2 Corinthians 5:18-19). The first place we are invited to practice this reconciliation is with one another. Forgiveness is a gift we receive and a gift we give. When we do, our communities become like our God—good and beautiful.

Experiencing Reconciliation

Reconciliation and forgiveness can be made real in our lives through practices that embed the story of Jesus into our lives. There are three soul-training exercises I recommend you try this week. Choose at least one, the one that best fits where you are right now, but try all three, if possible.

THREE EXERCISES

1. Allowing others to forgive **for you.** If you have been harmed greatly by someone, it may be impossible for you to forgive that person. You may not even be in a place where you *want* to forgive them, even though you feel you should. This is where community can be of great help. Those who stand with you in fellowship under the cross can begin to offer prayers of forgiveness for that person.

Here is how it works:

- Identify the person you would like to forgive but are not quite ready to forgive.

- Choose a close friend who is a Christ-follower and ask the person whether he or she would consider taking on that burden for you—the burden of your unforgiveness. Ask your friend to take that experience for you, *to bear this burden for you* (Colossians 3:13).

- If that person agrees, then he or she will commit to setting aside ten minutes each day to pray for the person and also for you, asking God to deepen your awareness of your own forgiveness.

Allowing our brothers and sisters in Christ to forgive where we cannot forgive may be a way for us to begin learning how to forgive. Knowing someone else is taking on the burden is freeing in itself. One member of our apprentice group allowed another person in our group to take on this burden for him. He said, "Just knowing that Laura is praying for this person and for me takes the pressure off of me. I feel as if the grip of unforgiveness is starting to loosen."

Another member of the group chose to do this with her spiritual director. She set up a time on a Saturday morning to talk about this situation, and her director agreed to do this exercise with her. She said that just by making the arrangements she was on the road to healing.

2. Steps to forgiving someone who has hurt you. It may be that you feel ready to try to forgive someone yourself. If so, there are some steps that may help in the process.

- *Identity.* I have been saying that the key to forgiveness is an awareness of your own forgiveness. This will entail deep reflection on Bible passages that announce your forgiveness. Either memorize or meditate on the following passage. It is a great proclamation of our new identity, our reconciliation and the motive to announce reconciliation to others:

  > If anyone is in Christ, there is a new creation: everything old has passed away; see, everything has become new! All this is from God, who reconciled us to himself through Christ, and has given us the ministry of reconciliation; that is, in Christ God was reconciling the world to himself, not counting their trespasses against them, and entrusting the message of reconciliation to us. (2 Corinthians 5:17-19)

- *Perspective.* I have found it helpful to pray for the person I am trying to forgive. This usually helps me get a new awareness of the person and his or her situation. Many times, through the leading of the Spirit, I am given a new understanding of that person and his or her life situation. One of the best phrases you can reflect on is this: *Hurt people hurt.*

This is a universal truth. People who hurt others are people who are themselves hurting because they have been hurt. I remember being angry and upset about a person who had said bad things about me in a meeting where I was not present. I spent the next two months thinking about ways to hurt the person back—in a Christian way, of course! I rehearsed conversations wherein I would reduce the person to tears through the power of my tongue.

Then I decided that, as an apprentice, there might be a better way! I began praying for this person and asking God to give me insight into his life. Not long after, I was visiting with someone who knows this person who explained—without my prompting—the extraordinary struggle and pain in his life. Realizing that this person probably hurt me in response to his own pain helped minimize the need I felt to hurt in return.

3. If your church offers the Lord's Supper, see something new in it. Many churches have Communion, or the Lord's Supper, on a regular basis. If your church offers this, I would encourage you to approach this means of grace with new eyes. The center of the Lord's Supper is the reminder that Christ has reconciled the world to himself. L. Gregory Jones puts it this way: "Christ's sacrifice relocates our lives as forgiven betrayers, as reconciled sinners, in communities of broken yet restored communion."

Reflect on these wonderful truths as you partake: Jesus is relocating your life, renarrating your life, and this meal is a tangible experience of that.

In an earlier exercise in this book I asked you to spend time with God using "two-by-four," that is, two hours with God and four acts of kindness. This exercise fits perfectly with that concept. Perhaps you could show up at church well ahead of time—thirty minutes or so, just to be quiet and to reflect on the act of worship. You may want to read 2 Corinthians 5:17-19 several times as you sit silently in the sanctuary or chapel.

the encouraging community

Tom Smith is a peculiar person, and a peculiar pastor—in the best sense of the word. His story is also peculiar. Ten years ago he was on "the fast track" in ministry in Johannesburg, South Africa. As a young man he was a quite talented minister and rose quickly through the ranks, being groomed to one day lead a large, successful congregation. He soon had a prestigious position at a megachurch.

Unfortunately he was also burning out. Ministry had become a job, a task, and was not fulfilling. Tom and his wife spent time praying and discerning what to do. They decided to get off the fast track to success and spend time learning what it means to be a Christ-follower and to be part of a community of Christ-followers.

They sold all they had and took a sabbatical in the United States. Tom was searching to see if he had anything left for ministry and for the church. During his time of rest and reflection, a new passion emerged from within. He caught a vision for a new way of approaching community and then returned to South Africa to let God lead in a new and risky way. The following is his description of the community they created: the Claypot Church.

In November 2003 a few pilgrims prayed together, searching for God's direction for them as a community. We searched for a biblical metaphor that would inform the rhythms of our group. After a few weeks of study and discerning God's voice together we landed on 2 Corinthians 4. In this passage Paul talks about us as jars of clay, and Christ the treasure: "But we have this treasure in jars of clay to show that this all-surpassing power is from God and not from us."

The metaphor grabbed us and we chose it as our biblical informant. We searched for a clay pot to serve as a visual reminder. After some vigorous searching, and after discovering how ridiculously overpriced pots were, we found the perfect pot. It was a discarded pot at a nursery that was filled with mud and had a few chips.

At the conclusion of one of our services we placed the pot in a big bag and broke it on the concrete floor. It symbolized our brokenness; everyone in the community took a broken piece home. All of us wrote a prayer on our shards and we came together to reassemble the pot. Although the pot is glued together, it still isn't a picture of perfection. Yet when we put a candle in it, it radiated a glorious light.

Tom and his people did not simply want to build a big church, they wanted to *be* the church, for one another and their community. Tom asked everyone in the community to make the following commitments in order to keep this light shining. He calls it responding to six invitations:

1. "Plug in" with God each day, either through prayer, Bible reading or other spiritual exercises.

2. Have three "bread breaking" times a week with each other as well as with those who don't know Christ.

3. Ask not "What is my spiritual gift?" but "How am I a gift to this community?" and offer your giftedness to the community.

4. Develop a friendship with someone who is different than you (race, religion, class, etc.).

5. Develop a servant mentality—downward mobility—wherein you seek to distribute your life's resources (time, treasure, talent) to those in need.

6. Discover a healthy rhythm in the way you use your time—margin, sabbath, not exceeding fifty hours at work.

What do you see as the distinction between the two questions in invitation 3? How would understanding this affect your life?

In addition, each member made one very important commitment that would help him or her keep these commitments. Tom explains:

> Every member teams up with at least one other family member in order to keep one another accountable. This accountability serves as an encouragement and sounding board for the rule of life in our community. We recommend that accountability partners meet at least monthly in order to stir one another up in love and good deeds (Hebrews 10:24-25).

There is one more peculiar practice in this community. Each year at the end of December Tom asks the people to begin a time of discernment for the entire month of January. Tom jokingly likes to say, "For the whole month of January I am the pastor of a church of *none*." The people are asked to search and discern where God is calling them. If they are led to return to Claypot for another year, they are asked to come on the last Sunday in January, when they meet to break a new jar, hand out the pieces, have each person write a prayer on their piece and then reassemble it the following Sunday.

The story of Claypot reveals the importance of commitment and accountability—two things that are becoming increasingly scarce in the Christian life. They are not a large church—less than a hundred—but they are being shaped as a people into Christlikeness. As our churches lower the bar of expectation and commitment, Clay-pot Church dares to raise it. They are standing in opposition to a false narrative held by many in our pews and perpetuated by many in our pulpits.

FALSE NARRATIVE:
THE COMMUNITY SERVES MY NEEDS

When we hear the terms *rule of life* or *covenants* we often write them off as unnecessary and legalistic. This is because of a false and pervasive narrative: The community exists to serve me and my needs. The community should not tell me what to do—that is up to me.

> Do you agree with the author that commitment and accountability are rare for contemporary churches? Why or why not?

We live in a consumer culture. Each day we are treated as a customer, and this leads us to believe we are entitled to have all of our needs met. We have become spoiled. The modern ethos of narcissism is pervasive in our culture and prevalent in our churches. The phenomenon of "church shopping" reveals our comfort with the consumer narrative. It is also revealed when we are treated as something other than consumers. Several years ago I was speaking with a group of pastors about this false narrative, and one of them had a story that illustrates this. "A year ago I felt called by God to encourage our people to read the Bible more," he said. "I challenged them, from the pulpit, to read the Bible for an hour each week. Not all at once, but perhaps for ten to twenty minutes on different occasions. After offering this challenge on several Sundays, a woman who had been in the church for several years came up to me and said, 'Pastor, I want you to know that I am leaving the church.' I asked why, and she said, 'Because when I joined this church, reading the Bible was not in the contract.' "

While it may be true that treating churchgoers as consumers by trying to meet their stated needs may make them feel more comfortable, by lowering our expectations of them as active participants we are decreasing the possibility of genuine transformation. We may end up with a massive church campus, but we will not end up with people who are being formed in Christlikeness. That entails a commitment the average consumer is not likely to make.

TRUE NARRATIVE: THE COMMUNITY SHAPES MY LIFE

The good and beautiful community is not made of merely comfortable Christians but Christlike men and women growing in their life with God and each other. In order to become that kind of community we need a new narrative, a biblical narrative, to reshape our behavior. Here is the true narrative regarding the rights and responsibility of the community: *The community exists to shape and guide my soul. The community has a right to expect certain behavior from me, and can provide the encouragement and accountability I need.*

From the beginning the *ecclesia* of Jesus has practiced soul shaping through many means: corporate worship, the breaking of bread, the teaching of the apostles, corporate fasting and holding each other accountable to live godly lives. Transformation into Christlikeness has been the aim and responsibility of the church from its beginning (Hebrews 10:24-25).

If the church has that *responsibility*, it also has the *right* to encourage certain behaviors from its members. We can and must offer forgiveness and reconciliation to all who seek it, and accept all who are broken and dysfunctional. But acceptance does not mean we ask nothing of the people who join our community. I realize that this approach causes uneasiness.

> Our uneasiness comes from seeing too much abuse in power. How have you seen this at work in the church?

We are reluctant to ask people to take a stand against sin, hesitant to challenge them to develop a prayer life and not inclined to telling people what to do in general. Some of the uneasiness is good, I think, because we need to have a healthy fear of being controlling or manipulative, or of abusing power.

Though these concerns are real, they do not mitigate our responsibility to encourage certain behaviors from the members of our community. The good and beautiful community has the responsibility and thus the right to lead people into godliness, which is the same thing as wholeness.

The soul-shaping role of the church is not just for our own spiritual nurture—it is meant to propel us out into mission. We gather together to worship, and in doing so we learn our ancient family language, tell our family narratives and enact our sacred moments. We also listen to the Spirit speak to us through sermon and song. In so doing we are shaped into a people, a community being transformed into goodness by our God who alone is good. But then we are sent. We leave worship as all new people, inspired by our connection to one another and to the old, old story. We leave to go out and, quite simply, change the world. We change it by our very presence. We cannot help but make a difference because we are the aroma of the resurrected Christ to a world that knows only death. We also behave differently, unselfishly, generously, and in so doing preach without saying a word. And of course we do preach when the time is right, ready with the right word in due season, telling our story of hope to those who hunger for it. We are shaped, and we are sent. We cannot have one without the other.

I want a community who will take an interest in my well-being, a community who is not afraid to ask me to make a commitment to my own spiritual growth and service to others, a community who dares to offer me a reliable pattern of transformation and then backs it up by challenging me to enter into some form of accountability in order to help me meet our commitments. I want a community who will challenge me to become who I already am: one in whom Christ dwells and delights, a light to the world, salt to the earth, the aroma of Christ to a dying world. I want a community who reminds me of who I am and will watch over me with love—which means offering both comfort and warning—so that I might live a life worthy of my calling.

But how do we do this without being judgmental and legalistic? How do we do this in the spirit of the One who loves us without condition and offers forgiveness and reconciliation no matter what we have done? How can we be both comforting and challenging at the same time? I believe it entails three things: (1) reminding each other who we are, (2) showing each other what we can be and (3) having the courage to hold each other accountable.

THE COMMUNITY REMINDS US WHO WE ARE

On a particularly challenging week I decided to skip church. I was tired from traveling and grading papers, and I rationalized my absence by reminding God of all the good work I had done for him that week. I had gone to a chapel service earlier in the week, and that was the final rationale I needed to sleep in and not feel guilty about missing church. Then my wife reminded me that it was the Sunday our son was getting his Bible presented to him for completing confirmation class. There would be no sleeping in. So I got ready, and we piled into the car as we do nearly every Sunday of the year.

We settled in to our usual spot in the sanctuary, and the service began. Early in the service we sang one of my favorite hymns, "Blessed Assurance," which begins:

Blessed assurance, Jesus is mine!
O what a foretaste of glory divine!
Heir of salvation, purchase of God,
Born of his Spirit, washed in his blood.

Then comes the chorus:

This is my story, this is my song,
Praising my Savior all the day long;
This is my story, this is my song,
Praising my Savior all the day long.

In a gentle way I was being reminded of my identity. This is my story: I have the blessed assurance that Jesus is my Savior; I am an inheritor of salvation; I was redeemed by God; I am born of the Spirit, and I am cleansed by the blood of Jesus.

That is the metanarrative that has become my story, the story Jesus has written me into and has written into me. It forms my identity. I know who I am: loved, forgiven, cleansed, made alive and destined for eternal joy. As we sing, the community reminds me who I am. The community has this power. We are bound by a common story, and as we tell it we are reminded of our true identity. In the epistle to the Hebrews, the author tells the people who they are: "we have been made holy through the sacrifice of the body of Jesus Christ once for all" (Hebrews 10:10 NIV).

> Dietrich Bonhoeffer affirms community's impact on the individual, saying, "The Christian needs another Christian who speaks God's Word to him. He needs him again and again when he becomes uncertain and discouraged." When have you experienced these moments in your own life and community?

The death and resurrection of Jesus was an atoning sacrifice for those who believe. Just as the sacrifice of a bull or a goat took away the sin of the individual or group, so the sacrifice of Jesus—the Lamb of God—took away the sins of the world. Those who gather in his name are a sanctified community, made holy through his sacrifice. We are set apart from the ways of this world. We are the *ecclesia*—those who have been *called out* from the world. We are the light of the world, the salt of the earth, a city set on a hill.

This is why Paul boldly addressed his letters to the "holy ones" or referred to them as "saints" (from the same Greek root word for holy, *hagios*). In fact, he addressed nearly all of his letters in this manner:

To the saints and faithful brothers and sisters in Christ in Colossae. (Colossians 1:2)

Paul and Timothy, servants of Christ Jesus,
  To all the saints in Christ Jesus who are in Philippi, with the bishops and deacons. (Philippians 1:1)

He called them "saints" because those who have put their confidence in Jesus and follow him as their Lord and Savior are holy—even when they know that their behavior does not match their identity. In a sense, we already *are* holy, and yet we are learning how to *be* holy.

We have been made holy by the work of Jesus, but our behavior often betrays our true identity. We are fallen, broken, prone to wander and to leave the God we love. Paul made this bold statement: "all have sinned and fall short of the glory of God" (Romans 3:23). Holy yet broken. That is a part of our identity. And that is another reason I like the practice of the Claypot Church. They break the jar and give a piece of it to each person. When the jar is reassembled it is not perfect—no church or community is—but the earthen vessel contains the treasure, which is Christ, whose light can shine out of our brokenness. In some ways he shines best through our brokenness, when we have allowed God to heal and restore us.

Holy yet broken. Broken yet holy. Broken yet able to carry the presence and power of Christ. This balance is important. There are churches that stress holiness in terms of certain behaviors. Taking their eyes off Jesus and focusing on rules, they become judgmental and hypocritical. There are other communities where the call to be holy is never heard. The good and beautiful community of appren-

Take a few minutes and write down "Holy yet broken. Broken yet holy" in your journal. Reflect on the seeming inconsistency these phrases offer, and then write about how they really do fit together.

tices of Jesus must keep this balanced awareness: we are holy, we are broken, and we are called to live holy and godly lives. The community reminds us who we are. They tell the story we need to hear repeatedly. Our memory is not that good, and the world we live in is telling us a different story. Only the community of Christ-followers has the truth we need to hear.

THE COMMUNITY SHOWS US WHAT WE CAN BECOME

We not only need to be reminded of who we are but also to be challenged to reflect that identity in our daily lives. This involves encouragement, admonishment and watching over one another in love. A good and beautiful community creates an ethos in which people are encouraged to engage in specific activities on a regular basis (some daily, some weekly, some ongoing) in order to become the people we truly are. This means setting high expectations. Each member should be asked to engage in growth-producing activities, from time alone with God to making friends with people outside our comfort zone to meeting monthly with an "encouragement" partner.

In short, the church is asking the people to reflect the glory that is already theirs. We are strengthened when we plug into God. Christ, who dwells in us, reveals himself in the breaking of bread, just as he did on the road to Emmaus. The Spirit who leads us uses our unique abilities as gifts to other apprentices. Those who stand in the strength of the kingdom naturally offer their resources to those who are in need.

These are not laws but opportunities for us to be who we are called to be. It is what we naturally do. Christians are a new creation, with new capacities. We can now interact with the Ruler of the universe. We have the joy of making deep connections with people—Christian or not. We are partakers of the divine nature (2 Peter 1:4), and our lives are meant to be gifts to others. We live under a new economic system: kingdom economics. What we share we never lose. These are not obligations but invitations to live out our calling.

We should approach these exercises as opportunities, and thus with excitement and joy. My dog gets excited when she thinks she might be going for a walk. If I walk into the room in tennis shoes, she starts to shake with excitement. If I reach for the leash, she goes crazy. I can hardly get her leash on because she is jumping around with unspeakable joy. We can do this only when we are reminded who we are and taught how these things work. I love the way Paul encouraged the Christians at Rome: "I myself feel confident about you, my brothers and sisters, that you yourselves are full of goodness, filled with all knowledge, and able to instruct one another" (Romans 15:14). He believed in them and called them to live that out. The community is empowered to tell us who we are and to challenge us as to what we can become.

One of my favorite verses is found in Hebrews. It offers a clear call to challenge one another to live as apprentices of Jesus: "Let us consider how to provoke one another to love and good deeds, not neglecting to meet together, as is the habit of some, but encouraging one another" (Hebrews 10:24-25). Notice the phrase "let us consider." We need to think about how we could *encourage* our fellow Christ-followers—literally, "provoke one another"—to love and good deeds. We need people around us who can encourage us to become the kinds of people Christ has called us to be.

THE COMMUNITY IS UNAFRAID
TO HOLD US ACCOUNTABLE

All of this sounds good on paper, but in real life this kind of enterprise involves many ups and downs, successes and failures, happy surprises and deep disappointments. Accountability involves the art of encouragement and admonishment. Encouragement is needed when we begin to lose sight or strength to keep fighting the good fight. We need someone in our corner to strengthen and encourage us, just as Paul and his fellow workers did when they visited the churches Paul had planted: "They returned to Lystra, then on to

Iconium and Antioch. There they strengthened the souls of the disciples and encouraged them to continue in the faith" (Acts 14:21-22). In the next chapter of Acts, Judas and Silas do the same: "Judas and Silas, who were themselves prophets, said much to encourage and strengthen the believers" (Acts 15:32).

Encouragement is an indispensable part of accountability. We often think of accountability as a negative thing, as an interaction of tough love. But in reality it is as much about the art of encouragement as it is about the art of keeping high expectations. There is so much in life that beats us down and discourages us that we need a steady dose of encouragement. We each need a fellow Christ-follower who is absolutely convinced that we are great and can do great things. We each need fellow apprentices who applaud us when we succeed and pull us up when we fail.

Encouragement also entails admonishment. To admonish is to warn, to watch out for and to offer guidance to another. Paul told the Colossians, "Let the word of Christ dwell in you richly; teach and admonish one another in all wisdom" (Colossians 3:16).

When we open our lives to another, we do so with the expectation that he or she will freely offer us a word of warning when we need it. I was in an accountability group with four other men, and we met weekly to share what was going on in our lives. It was quite common for one of us to challenge someone who needed it. This was never done maliciously or with a hint of meanness. Quite the opposite; it was done carefully, and with love.

For example, at one point I had accepted several speaking engagements, and while the ministry work was good, it was taking a toll on several other areas of my life. The guys could see I was tired, and they heard guilt in my voice when I spoke about having to be away from my family, especially when our kids were small. One of the guys said gently, "Jim, I am not sure that you need to take every invitation you are offered. I think it is hurting your soul and your family, even though it is obvious you are doing good work." The others concurred.

Then we talked about working together to decide which engagements I would accept. We came up with a plan, and they offered to help me decide, through prayer, how I would respond. They stepped in, had the courage to admonish me and then offered to bear this burden with me. It was community at its best.

Holding someone accountable is not easy; it takes discernment. Paul told the Thessalonians to treat certain people in certain ways, fitting their condition: "We urge you, beloved, to admonish the idlers, encourage the faint hearted, help the weak, be patient with all of them" (1 Thessalonians 5:14). I love the verbs in this verse: *admonish, encourage, help* and *be patient*. This is the grammar of community. Certainly encouragement is necessary, as is helping others and being patient. Those are the characteristics of an apprentice of Jesus, and they are birthed only in community, not in isolation. But the first verb, *admonish* (warn), is not something many of us feel comfortable with. Still, it is a dimension of love.

What if my accountability group had chosen not to admonish me? What if they, out of fear of hurting my feelings, had simply looked the other way? They would not have been loving me, which by our definition is "to will the good of another." I understand the reservations: Will the person we admonish get angry? Will he or she leave the fellowship? What if my discernment is wrong? Those are good questions, but they must not prevent us from doing the hard but necessary work of admonishment. If we are to watch over one another in love, we will have to overcome our fear of speaking the truth to a fellow apprentice. Always, though, we must speak the truth in love.

A RADICAL METHOD

In the eighteenth century the early Methodists were one of the purest examples of the power of accountability in community. The leader, John Wesley, preached to countless people, and thousands were converted. John was encouraged to preach outdoors to the masses by his longtime friend George Whitefield. Whitefield was, by most people's estimates, a far better preacher than Wesley. He preached to larger audiences and saw greater numbers of conversions than Wesley. But there was a difference in how they instructed people to live *after* conversion. Whitefield had no plan; he simply assumed that people who gave their life to Christ would find a church and live out the Christian life.

Wesley, on the other hand, insisted that people join what were called societies, which functioned very much like churches (though without Communion, as Wesley was a true Anglican and wanted people to attend an Anglican church as well). In these Methodist societies the people were encouraged to attend many times a week to hear the preaching of Wesley or one of his other ministers. In addition, they were asked to join a class, which consisted of twelve people and a class leader. Each week they were challenged to come to the class meeting to share candidly with one another about the state of their souls. Wesley was so serious about this that if people failed to attend the class meeting, they would not be allowed to return unless they came to him and shared why they were absent.

Though Wesley's practice might not work in today's world, it certainly did in his time. He offered people a *method* (hence the name Methodists) to grow in Christlikeness in the context of communities. The movement spread rapidly and continued to grow in astounding numbers. He asked a lot of his people, but he saw a lot of transformation. The Methodist movement stands as one of the great movements in the church. The work of Wesley continued on through many generations. George Whitefield, however, left no such legacy. While considered one of the greatest preachers, Whitefield never started a movement.

In one stark entry in Wesley's journal, he commented on a time when he failed to establish societies and classes in a region where he had preached. He returned twenty years after a great revival in a region called Pembrokeshire and was grieved to see that no evidence of their evangelistic success remained. He concluded,

> I was more convinced than ever that the preaching like an apostle, without joining together those that are awakened and training them up in the ways of God, is only begetting children for the murderer. How much preaching has there been for these twenty years all over Pembrokeshire! But no regular societies, no discipline, no order or connection. And the consequence is that nine in ten of those once awakened are now faster asleep than ever.

Though "begetting children for the murderer" is quite harsh, it shows how important *discipline, order* and *connection* were to Wesley. And they should be to us as well.

CHALLENGING THOSE WHO ARE READY

I know three things from experience. First, people rise to the level of expectation. We fail because we do not ask for accountability and commitment. Second, people intuitively know that when things are made easy there is little chance that any good will come from it. We lower our expectations because we think people will respond in greater numbers, but in reality we do them no service, and most people sense this. Third, while not everyone in every church is ready to make a commitment to transformation, there are many who are ready and are not being challenged. Far too much attention is being paid to getting people to come to church, and far too little is paid to those who are hungering for a deeper life with God.

When I first started teaching material in The Apprentice Series, I stood before our congregation and offered an *anti*-pitch pitch to the people. I said, "I am looking for people who are serious about their life with God and are willing to make a commitment—a steep commitment. I am asking for thirty weeks of your life—a few hours each week to read the material and engage in the soul-training exercises, and then to come each Sunday to gather as a group to share how we are doing. You can only miss three of our sessions together. If you cannot make that commitment, then I encourage you not to apply. If you are serious, I need you to write an essay telling me why you want to enter this program. I will read your essay and let you know if you have been accepted."

Many of the people later told me they were shocked. No one had ever stood up and offered such a challenge. Many felt intimidated. But over forty people wrote essays in order to get in the twenty-five open spots. Those selected came to the group with a lot of excitement, as if they had been selected to do something important. The commitment level was high; the people read, engaged in the exercises and came to the group ready to share. Every person in the group experienced lasting change. I took this same approach for the next three years, ultimately taking over one hundred people through the program. The impact on individual lives, as well as on our church, was evident.

Dallas Willard believes that in any given church approximately 10 percent of the people are ready to grow and willing to make an effort to make it happen. He thinks the church puts too much emphasis on trying to light a fire under the 90 percent, and neglects to challenge the 10 percent who are sitting idle but wanting help. Dallas theorizes that if we challenged the 10 percent, they would grow and subsequently would begin to effect change in others. This method, he believes, has been used by all of the great leaders in Christian history, including the most important of all, Jesus himself. Jesus invested heavily in a small band of followers, who in turn changed the world.

I do, however, want to offer one warning that comes from my experience in churches: the "80/20 rule." That is, 80 percent of a church's work is done by 20 percent of the people. There are people who are natural servers, natural doers, who will respond to every call to serve. We tend to take advantage of those who are willing to do whatever is asked. This almost always leads to burnout. We need to challenge the entire community to be involved. Many churches do not ask enough of everyone, and therefore ask too much of only a few, often those who have trouble saying no.

In many of our communities, service is reduced to doing things for the good of the church (e.g., serving on a committee, helping out with activities and events). This is one way to serve, but there are many others. Sometimes we feel as if service to the church is more important than service to the sick and needy. Service is an aspect of discipleship, but service itself is not discipleship. The current arrangement puts too much pressure on a few people to engage in specific acts of service to the church, which ends up overextending those few while the rest sit on the sidelines. In place of the 80/20 rule we need to encourage the entire community to engage in a balanced and comprehensive pattern of apprenticeship where everyone is involved.

A YEAR OF ENCOURAGEMENT

One summer I spent two weeks working with Dallas Willard, assisting him in a class he was teaching on spirituality and ministry. We had long talks about formation and the difficulties faced in growing as apprentices of Jesus. We concluded that a key is to have someone standing with us who will hear the state of our soul, someone who will push us to be who we want to be and will be there in the end to ask, "How are you doing?" A moment of silence hung in the air. I wanted to ask Dallas if he would be willing to do that for me. Then I realized that I should offer to do the same for him. The thought of asking my wise, Christlike mentor, "Dallas, would you mind baring your soul to me and letting me hold you accountable?" seemed ludicrous.

Which is why I did it. And amazingly, he agreed without hesitation. We were driving to an airport and had about thirty minutes in the car, and another forty-five in the airport. During that time he shared the areas of his life that needed a little nudge, and I did the same. My need for nudging far exceeded his, but you get the idea. We agreed to hold each other in prayer for a year, and every time we saw each other we would ask how we were doing. We ended up being in the same place three times over the year, and we never failed to ask how our plan was working.

Knowing that Dallas knew what I wanted to do and that he was counting on me to stand with him in prayer and encouragement helped me that year. I was able to make some real strides in a few areas, and believe it or not, Dallas did as well. It showed me that no matter who we are, no matter how deeply we live in the kingdom, we still need to be encouraged, admonished and challenged to grow in Christlikeness; we need to be accountable to an encouraging community.

Finding an Accountability Friend

This week, find a person who can encourage you and watch over you in love. I recommend you find someone within your small group or church (if you are involved in one). If not, seek out a trusted friend. It may be your spouse, though this is not recommended. It is probably better to ask a good friend, someone who would not be terribly surprised at being asked to do the following exercise with you.

The key here is finding someone you feel safe with. You will discuss the state of your soul with this person, so it is imperative that you feel comfortable with this person. If you sense that this person might judge you or react to what you say in an unloving way, then choose someone else.

Once you have chosen this person, be sure to make clear what you want from him or her. It is not necessary for the person to reciprocate; you are not asking your friend to bare his or her soul with you, but to ask you some questions and listen, and to offer some encouragement or admonishment if necessary.

When you meet, use the following questions. Be sure that your partner asks them of you, and if they're comfortable, you ask the same questions of your friend:

1. How is your soul?

2. In what ways do you need to be encouraged right now?

3. What, if anything, is holding you back from living more fully for
God?

These are great questions. They elicit a lot of good responses. And
if you answer them openly and honestly, it will lead to some very
fruitful discussion.

If the person is simply there to ask you these questions and not
to answer them in return, do not be surprised if he or she decides
to answer them anyway—especially if you model transparency.
People long to know and be known, and when they feel safe they
will usually share a great deal. We live in an age of much talking
but little listening. If you show a willingness to listen, be prepared to do so. People are hungering for a safe place to share from
their depths.

That said, be careful about what and how much you share. Unless you have a long-standing relationship and have done this kind
of thing with this person, you cannot be sure of his or her reaction.
Should you share something shocking, this exercise could turn out
badly. A good rule of thumb is to share only what you think the
person can handle. Should you need to share something deeper and
more painful, I would encourage you to seek out a pastor or a men-
tal-health-care professional, because they are trained to deal with
information or problems that others are not trained to understand.

Above all, be at peace. If this is the first time you are doing something like this, do not enter into it with a great deal of worry and
concern. This exercise is designed to be a gift, not a burden. Approach it with an attitude of joyful expectancy. If it becomes uncomfortable, keep the discussion at a more informal level. It may take
time to develop trust with this person. Again, be at peace. You cannot rush these kinds of interactions. If, however, you are able to find
it—now or down the road—you have found a treasure more valuable
than gold.

One other concern: when choosing your partner within an exist-
ing group, be mindful of the fact that this can lead to hurt feelings.

Someone may not be asked to be anyone's partner. Try to be sensitive to this, and if necessary, ask that person to be your partner—it is all right to have more than one.

seven

The Generous community

The church meeting was interrupted by a woman who said, "Pastor Jim, there is a man on the phone who really needs to speak to you."

"Can it wait till the meeting ends? Can I call him back?" I asked.

"He sounds pretty desperate," she said, her face looking very concerned.

I told her I would take it.

"Can I help you?" I asked the person on the other end of the phone.

"Yes, please. Pastor, I need your help. I have not eaten in three days. Can you please give me some money to eat?"

"No, I cannot give you money," I said, "but I can take you to a place and pay for some food for you."

He seemed truly grateful. I asked where he was and told him I would be there in ten minutes. He was not in a safe part of town, but it was still light outside, a little after six in the evening. I must be honest: *I was dreading going to help this man*. I was scared about going to that part of town by myself, picking up a stranger and possibly being exploited. It had been a long day, and I just wanted to go home, take off my shoes and watch television. Something in me pulled me along, though, and I decided not to let him down, whoever he was.

As I drove, I thought about all of the times I had been ripped off by people who called or came to the church saying they needed money, all with sad and sympathy-inducing stories. After being exploited a few times by people who took my money and used it for something other than what they said they needed, I became jaded. That is why I told the young man on the phone that I would take him to dinner and not just hand him money.

> Seeing a destitute/homeless person panhandling isn't unusual for most of us, sadly, but journal about a time you especially recall. What stood out to you? What thoughts were you weighing as you decided whether to give?

When I picked him up he was scruffy and skinny, and he looked a little sick. He did not smell very good, either. We went to a buffet restaurant, and he ate enough to feed a small army. I noticed he had a slight German accent, though he did not speak much. He was practically inhaling his food. On the drive back he told me he had been in America for a couple of months staying with some friends, but he had worn out his welcome and had hitchhiked, ending up in Wichita.

After dinner I drove him back to the discount hotel where he was staying. When he got out, he thanked me for the meal. He asked me for my name and the church's name, wrote them down, and after a handshake got out of the car with a very full belly. I drove home with mixed feelings. On one hand I was feeling good, but on the other hand I was still wondering if I had done the right thing. Was I part of some scam? Surely taking a very hungry person to dinner can only be a good thing. But what if he had a bag of money inside of his room and was just using me? Or what if he had money and used it to buy drugs? I felt very unsettled about the matter. I decided to let it go and trust God. Still, I went to bed that night confused about the right and the wrong in these situations.

THREE FALSE NARRATIVES: JUDGMENT, SCARCITY AND ENTITLEMENT

Truth be told, I did not want to help this young man because of my prejudice. He was from another country, he was dirty and smelly, and he had been staying in a bad part of town, all of which meant I could stereotype him, giving me a clear excuse *not* to be generous. Yes, I did help this young man, but many other times I refused to help someone in need. I have since discovered that I refused to help because I held three narratives that, when combined, allowed me to turn from those in need without guilt: a judgmental narrative, an entitlement narrative and a scarcity narrative. When they are all adopted (and they usually are), the person living by these narratives will almost never become a generous person.

God helps those who help themselves. The first narrative is well known: "God helps those who help themselves." Many people actually believe this is from the Bible. It is not. It is from an edition of *Poor Richard's Almanac*, written by Ben Franklin in 1757. Franklin was not a Christian, but a deist. He said a lot of really brilliant things, but this was not one of them. This judgmental narrative is a bulwark against generosity, a sturdy protection against the need to help those who are in need. God, it appears, only helps those who pull themselves up, get their act together and put in hard work. If *God* will not help these lazy people, then I am also off the hook. Instead of feeling guilty, I can look at those who are in need and judge them. Judging makes our guilt go away.

But we can also use our well-being as a means of thinking that we have done something to deserve it. If things are going well, we can assume that somehow we have done something to deserve it. This is the flip side of our false narrative about justice—somehow our condition must be tied to our good works. While it is true that engaging in sin leads to the destruction of our souls, it may not lead to immediate catastrophe in the rest of our lives. The Scriptures remind us repeatedly not to envy those who are sinful and yet prosper. And we ought not judge those who are in dire straights. Though it may be due to sin, laziness and bad decisions, those who are in a bad situation may not always be directly responsible for it.

Which of the three narratives that prevent generosity do you find yourself falling captive to? Why do you think this is so?

If I give it away, I have less. There is a second narrative that prevents generosity: If I give it away I will have less. This scarcity narrative is built on the idea that whatever I give away is now lost, whatever I share is gone and whatever I provide for another contributes to my own lack. In one sense this is true. If I give you some of my cookie, for example, there will be less of it for me. It is simple math: take away any amount and the original amount is reduced. It couples well with the next false antigenerosity narrative, the one of entitlement.

What I have is mine to use for my own pleasure. The most significant narrative that prevents generosity is, What I have is mine to use for my own pleasure. This entitlement narrative teaches us that the things that we possess, whether money, time or abilities, are ours to use as we see fit, which often means using them for our own gain and not the benefit of others. If I start with the notion that what I have is mine, that I somehow earned it or deserve it, then I am entitled to use it any way I want. It falls under my discretion; I get to choose when, how and how much I give.

All three of these narratives come together to form a mighty fortress against generosity. In order to discover the truth, we need to examine the Bible's narratives. Here, we discover that these narratives are not only wrong, they are also the opposite of the truth and do not lead to the good life or the good community we are seeking.

TRUE NARRATIVES:
HELPLESSNESS, PROVISION AND STEWARDSHIP

God helps those who cannot help themselves. Like all false narratives, the "God helps those who help themselves" contains some truth; God *does* help those who are able to help themselves, but God also helps those who *cannot* help themselves. The Gospels are a *Who's Who* of helpless, broken, despised people, yet God *helps* them: the woman caught in adultery, dead Lazarus, Peter making promises he cannot keep. In fact, it would be easier to make the case that God helps the needy more than those who have plenty. Perhaps that is because those who are in need have open hands, and only open hands can receive. The prejudice narrative must be overcome if we are to become generous.

The Bible repeatedly reminds us that we are sinful and broken. The psalms consistently teach that humans are fallen, broken and wayward. If we are honest, we will admit our utter helplessness. Yes, we may have worked hard to earn a living, buy a home and put food on our table. But in truth we are contingent beings who rely on the mercy of God every single moment. Were it not for the air I breathe and the sun that produces life, I would not last a minute. None of us, in truth, can help ourselves. We are all in need. We are all helpless, and God graciously helps us. Ironically, he uses other humans to do this work.

> Reflect on the irony that God uses other humans to function as his hands, feet and heart toward one another. When have you experienced this for yourself, either as a giver or as a recipient?

If we all share, we all have enough. When the children of Israel wandered toward the Promised Land, they had no food. God provided food for them in the form of manna. They did not know what it was, and neither do we (the word *manna* literally means, "What is it?"). They soon discovered it was food that kept them alive. But they were not supposed to store it up. If they tried to store some for the next day, it rotted, thus teaching them to rely on God's provision each day. Another rule about manna-gathering is seldom taught but contains a deep truth about generosity. God commanded them to take only enough for their own sustenance, and no more. That way, there would be enough for everyone. They were told to measure how much to eat by using a measuring device, called an omer, which held about two quarts of manna (see Exodus 16:16-18).

Humans have a tendency to hoard, to take more than we need. Unfortunately, some people took more, and as a result some had to take less. But when they used the omer, everyone had all they needed, and there was no lack.

Why do we try to consume more than we need? Because we believe there will not be enough for everyone, so we need to take all that we can. This is a narrative of scarcity. The scarcity narrative, however, can be replaced by the *sharing* narrative once we realize the economy of the kingdom. The Omer Principle shows that *there is enough for everyone—but only when we take our fair share.* Hunger experts tell us that there is enough food on the planet to end world hunger, but some (mostly in the Western, developed world) consume more than they need, which leaves less for others. One night I was up late and watched an infomercial for a weight-loss program. For only $150 a month, I was told, I could lose a pound a day—only $5 a day. I switched channels and saw a relief organization commercial showing children with bloated stomachs, and was told that for $3 a day I could prevent a child from dying of hunger. The irony was not lost on me.

Of course, the Omer Principle is not meant to be mandatory or forced (as in communism). It then becomes not something good but evil. But when people arrive at omer-like decisions (Gee, maybe if I didn't buy this I could give more to that) by the leading of the Spirit, much good comes. God designed a world where there is enough for everyone, as long as we take only what we need.

What I have is God's, to use for his glory. In contrast to the narrative "What is mine is mine," the true narrative is "What appears to be mine is really God's." Nothing I have is mine—it is all a gift from God. We easily get duped into thinking that the things in our possession are ours, and that we therefore get to choose how to use them. In truth, God has designed human life in such a way that makes this illusion quite easy to believe. God has given each of us a little kingdom over which to say what happens. This is God's plan. He wants us to be stewards. So he gives us bodies, talents and money so we can produce good things.

In chapter six we saw how kingdom economics work differently than world economics. How would living under the idea of God's abundance versus our scarcity make a difference in your life?

But our little kingdoms are not our own. We are stewards of God's gifts; everything belongs to God. That changes everything. No longer can I say, "What is mine is mine to do with what I please." Instead, "What is mine is not really mine, but God's," and therefore I must ask, "How shall I use the gifts you have given me?" This fundamental shift affects all of our daily decisions.

Generosity is an attitude, an inward disposition, that spawns acts of self-sacrifice, which is how God acts toward us. My colleague Matt Johnson put it well:

Generosity is "other-centered," whereas greed is self-centered, which obviously is a different way of stating the third true narrative. When I'm thinking of myself first and myself alone, then I struggle to give anything to anyone. But on those *kingdom-focused days* when I'm thinking of God and God's provision and resources, it is simply a matter of connecting the resources I have been given with the needs and I get to be a conduit for this process.

A THEOLOGY OF ENOUGH

People go to extremes with money and possessions. Some preach a gospel of prosperity, based on the idea that the good life is about using money and possessions for our own happiness, which God will provide when we do the right things (for example, give to a certain ministry or say a special prayer for thirty days). On the other hand, some preach a gospel of poverty, teaching that the way to be truly spiritual is to be poor. Both extremes are dangerous. The prosperity gospel is simply greed covered in the veneer of religion. The poverty gospel is also dangerous. There is nothing spiritual about poverty, and no one is actually better for having become poor. Dallas Willard notes:

> The idealization of poverty *is one of the most dangerous illusions of Christians in the contemporary world.* Stewardship—which requires possessions and includes giving—is the true spiritual discipline in relation to wealth. . . .
>
> [I]n general, being poor is one of the poorest ways to help the poor.

Prosperity and poverty are not the only choices we have. Author and practitioner Shane Claiborne offers a third option: "We need a third way, neither the prosperity gospel nor the poverty gospel, but the Gospel of abundance rooted in a theology of enough."

A gospel of abundance is found only in the kingdom of God, where somehow we have what we need when we need it. The kingdom of God is not like an ATM where we can get an endless supply of resources to spend however we like. It is a dispenser of resources offered to those who understand the ways of the kingdom. Where there is a need and a person who can meet that need, the supply will never run out.

One of the great dangers in America, however, is complacency. We live in an affluent society whose values are skewed. A great question is, Where is the Spirit leading me as an individual and us as a community? This requires individual and corporate discernment. Most Western Christians are not pursuing either the gospel of poverty or the gospel of prosperity. The majority of Western Christians must wrestle with what a "theology of enough" means in a culture of excess. How will we discern what is enough? Who will make that decision? If we let our culture make the decision, I am afraid we will become like those who use buckets instead of omers.

For example, *Forbes* online magazine quantified how much money a person would need to "live well." Living well, they estimated *by their standard,* meant living in a four-thousand-square-foot home, owning a second home in a beautiful place (beach, mountain), three luxury automobiles, dinner once a week at an upscale restaurant, three vacations a year, private school for your children, upscale colleges when they graduate and a 1 percent savings rate. The bare minimum amount needed to finance this kind of life is two hundred thousand dollars annually, but in many cities that number goes up. If this is the standard of the *good life,* then it might make we who live on much less feel as if we are exempt from *giving* because we are not truly living—at least living well.

Discernment will mean asking, How is God leading me in the use of my financial resources? In light of the great need in our world, what is God calling me and my fellow apprentices to in terms of standard of living and material possessions? It will not necessarily mean that we will be asked to sell everything and live among the poor. But it does mean that we will look at our income and assets in a new light—one illuminated by the light of the kingdom of God.

PRIMARY AREAS OF STEWARDSHIP

Money and possessions are but one way we learn generosity. God has endowed us with several other capacities. The call to stewardship can be expressed by using five resources that are ours to share, if we are willing.

Soul. God has given us a soul, which has several capacities. By our soul we can think, reason, imagine, feel and remember. The *mind* and the *emotions* are essential aspects of the soul and incredible gifts to us. Through our souls we write poems and symphonies, design ways to improve life, solve problems that plague us, envision a better tomorrow, mourn the loss of others and grieve for our sin, and create memories that shape our lives and give them meaning. Our souls are magnificent gifts, to be used to bless others.

Body. God has also given us bodies, and these amazing organisms possess incredible capacities, such as sight, smell, hearing, touch and taste. Our bodies have hands to hold and grasp and hammer and write, and feet to take us to wonderful places. If you have ever lost some physical ability for any amount of time, you know well how precious these abilities are. Our bodies are given to us by God to be used to bring hope and healing to others.

Talent. Merely having a soul and a body is enough for us to live in gratitude to God, but he offers us more. We have also been given a measure of strength, health and physical attributes that are uniquely ours. Strength, health, beauty and influence are gifts from God. God has created us with unique talents and abilities, and they too are to be used to advance the cause of God.

Time. We have also been given the gift of time, even though in our day we complain about the lack of it. In truth, most of us have a lot of time in which to invest our energy and attention. Time, they say, is money. While that may be true, making money is not always the best use of our time. Very few will reach the end of their lives and wish they had made more money; rather, most of us will wish we had spent more time being present to those we love. My daughter Hope said to me one day recently, "Dad, will you play a game with me?" I was under a deadline to finish several projects, so the thought of playing an hour or two of Monopoly did not seem like a good use of my time. However, the Spirit whispered to me that I could not have spent that Saturday afternoon in a better way. So I stopped what I was doing and we played. She sparkled for that hour, and I repented. Time is a gift God gives to us to use well, mainly to spend on the things that are most important.

Treasure. We are stewards of our financial and material resources. Though we may have much or little, these monies are given to us to use for the good of others. Certainly we can and should take care of our basic costs, but that which we have beyond these costs should be used to bless others. Money is not evil, nor is it the root of evil. The *love* of money is the

> As with money, kingdom economics work differently in relation to time when we are Spirit led. How have you experienced this with your time?

root of all kinds of evil (1 Timothy 6:10). Money can be a great source of blessing. By it the naked are clothed, the hungry are fed, the needy are cared for, the sick are made well. The money we are able to generate can be used to make our communities better places.

A lot has been made of the extraordinary generosity of the early church found in Acts 2: "All who believed were together and had all things in common; they would sell their possessions and goods and distribute the proceeds to all, as any had need" (Acts 2:44-45).

Apprentices of Jesus need to carefully consider these verses because there are several common mistakes we can easily make. One is to take this summary statement as a model for all Christian communities and insist on it as the standard way of life. This is a mistake, I believe. First, the church did not continue this practice indefinitely. Second, enforcing it as the rule for all groups tends toward legalism. Third, while the ideal seems inviting, the actual practice of communal living is fraught with much frustration, as we see only a few chapters later: "Now during those days, when the disciples were increasing in number, the Hellenists complained against the Hebrews because their widows were being neglected in the daily distribution of food" (Acts 6:1). The problem of unequal distribution caused the disciples to have to step in and set up a new order to make sure people were treated fairly, which they did (see Acts 6:2-7). They decided to appoint people (called "deacons") to watch over the use of funds, allowing the disciples to focus on preaching and teaching.

But the other common mistake is to neglect the Acts 2 model entirely, dismissing it as a quaint practice that does not work for us today. Something similar may in fact work today, and some who live in intentional communities practice a variation of it with great success. While I am not called to this practice personally, I would rather err on the side of trying to make my goods available to others and giving all I can to those who are in need. In many of the great movements in the history of the church we see something similar to the Acts 2 model. I find these verses challenging for me personally.

I offer this practice, which I know works well: give all you can to organizations that are designed to distribute food, clothing and monies to those in need. In my city there are several organizations that do an excellent job of this. They are like the deacons in Acts 6. Their doors are open each day, and they know how to help people get what they need. More than that, they help people find jobs and offer other services that many local churches are not equipped to do.

A GENEROUS COMMUNITY

Giving is not simply an individual activity or one to be left to specialized organizations. Local church communities need to participate in the joy of giving. My own local church has taught me much about generosity. Chapel Hill United Methodist Church in Wichita has been a generous community from its inception, thanks to apprentices of Jesus who understand kingdom economics. From our earliest days we decided to give 10 percent of our income to be used directly for those in need, regardless of where they attend church (it is called the "First Fruits Fund"). A few years ago the sister of our youth pastor died, leaving the family unable to pay for her funeral and four children practically destitute. Our church not only paid for her fu-

neral (even though she did not attend the church), we also set up a
fund to help pay for clothing and schooling for the children.

Not long ago we had a visiting pastor come to our city for a sabbatical. He and his wife arrived in Wichita only to find that their
promised room and board had been taken away, due to unforeseen
circumstances. When the people in our church heard about their
situation, they quickly decided to use monies from the First Fruits
Fund to pay for their rent. Then, the people of the church held a
meeting to see what they could give by way of furniture. In less than
a day they had a fully furnished apartment, all because of the generosity of the people in a church community who had learned the
blessing of giving. Of course, countless churches do this, which is
good news. The community of Christ-followers are natural givers because they understand the economics of the kingdom.

THE MANY WAYS OF BEING GENEROUS

Jesus said it is more blessed to give than to receive (Acts 20:35). For
many of us, it is much more comfortable giving than receiving. Richard Foster once pointed out to me how difficult it is to allow ourselves
to be served, which he calls "the service of being served." This requires
an act of submission on our part. When others are generous, we feel a
need to repay their acts of generosity. I have learned to let others share
their gifts with me, and as I reflect on their generosity I have discovered that I am deeply blessed.
Let me offer some examples.

As you consider your own
talents and gifts, whose
community do you bless?
Who blesses your community?

ered that I am deeply blessed.
Let me offer some examples.

My wife, Meghan, con-
stantly blesses me with her
joy, enthusiasm for life and
belief in me. My son, Jacob,
is quiet, but he offers me the
gift of wonder each time I see him smile. My daughter Hope is a well-
spring of hope. I once told her that I write better when she is in my
study, doing one of her puzzles. She selflessly sits quietly by my side

doing her puzzles and stops to give me hugs every hour or so. Our daughter Madeline, though not with us in body, is present to me in the spirit, reminding me of the faithfulness of God and the power made perfect in weakness.

My friend Patrick is my ruthless protector who watches over me and my time and energy with care, and never fails to remind me who I am in Christ. My friend C. J. gives me constant encouragement and daily reminders that we live in the kingdom that is strong. My friend Matt offers me gentle wisdom and an ongoing example of Christlikeness. My friend Jimmy generously shares the strength that comes through struggle, and gently reminds me to look at what I have done, not what I have not. My friend Trevor is a true and trusted friend who allows me to be human; he gives me the gift of nonjudgmental friendship.

My friend Andrew offers his deep wisdom just when I need it, and always offers it in humility. My pastor, Jeff Gannon, delivers messages that inspire me. Though he is preaching to our congregation as a whole, I often feel as if he has been given a word just for me. My friends Bob and Arlo have given generously of their own money to support the ministry I am involved in. Their generosity astounds me, but when I try to share my appreciation, they simply tell me that God has given to them, so they want to give back to God. All of these people, and so many more I do not have space to mention, give generously of their gifts. It is not easy to do, but I am learning how to be thankful without feeling a need to repay them.

Sometimes the generosity of anonymous people is a blessing to us. Much of our daughter Madeline's short life on earth was spent in hospitals. I remember one time being profoundly exhausted from sitting on cold, vinyl chairs with nothing to eat or drink. A nurse told me about the Ronald McDonald Room down the hall. I walked into a room that looked like a room in someone's home. It had comfortable chairs, couches, a television, coffee and snacks. It became a welcome haven of rest for my wife and me to visit. I never knew the person or persons who gave of their time and money to create this space, but I am grateful that they used their resources to bless our family and many others.

A PLAN FOR BECOMING A GENEROUS COMMUNITY

Learn the joy of giving. I visited a church when they were having their annual Stewardship Sunday. I overheard a man after the service saying to a friend, "I hate it when the church talks so much about money. It makes me feel like all they want me for is my checkbook." I was so saddened to hear this. The pastor did not present his message in such a way as to make people feel like this. In fact, he repeatedly backed away from coming across this way. This man clearly did not understand the joy of giving. Somehow the narrative of the blessing of giving did not break through. I believe we need to teach and preach about the blessing of giving.

One of the best sermons on stewardship I ever heard was from my mentor and friend Reverend Jerry Vogt. He stood in the pulpit without any reservations and told about the many blessings he and his wife received through the years by their giving. It was not prideful in any way. He and his wife were simply being stewards of their resources. He never once used guilt, but by the time he finished my desire to give all I could was increased. This is true not only of money but of all our resources. We need to be reminded over and over of the joys of giving, and it is best delivered by those who speak from experience.

Learn the way to margin. In order to be generous, we must create *margin*. In order to give, we must first have something to give. "Margin" means taking in more than what goes out, thus allowing us to give. Most Americans have no margin, financial or otherwise. To say to them, "You need to give more time and money to those in need" when they are in this condition is unfair. They first have to create margin. The best way to create margin is *frugality*. I know that is a negative word for many, but we need to redeem it. It refers to responsible living, setting appropriate boundaries.

Frugality involves being very careful about our time and resources. Frugality is not the same as being stingy. It also does not mean being cheap. Those who practice frugality are not required to buy the cheapest version. Frugality means buying what we need, but not necessarily what we want. As Dallas Willard notes, "Practicing frugality means we stay within the bounds of what general good judgment would designate as necessary for the kind of life to which God has led us." Frugal spending decreases debt and moves us toward financial margin. Frugality with our time means learning to say no to some things so we can say yes to others. Until we have financial margin, generosity will be impossible.

> Do you agree that the narratives in the chapter enable you to practice frugality? Why or why not?

Learn ways to give. Many people have no idea where, when and how to give. We need to let people know of the many ways people can give. One church I know consistently lets people know about opportunities to serve with their time. For example, twice a month they have a "Parents' Day Out" for parents of handicapped children. And every Saturday they sponsor meals for the homeless. They also invest time and money in a depressed area of town. During the worship service, they inform people about the need and how they can participate.

DIVES AND LAZARUS: ONLY ONE CHANCE

We can only be stewards of these great capacities *in our lifetime on earth*. The moment we die, there will be no chance of offering our gifts of time, talents, abilities or possessions. One of the most haunting parables of Jesus is the story of a rich man (legend has named him Dives) and a poor man named Lazarus (not the Lazarus who was raised from the dead). Though the parable is lengthy, it is worth reading carefully:

There was a rich man who was dressed in purple and fine linen and who feasted sumptuously every day. And at his gate lay a poor man named Lazarus, covered with sores, who longed to satisfy his hunger with what fell from the rich man's table; even the dogs would come and lick his sores. The poor man died and was carried away by the angels to be with Abraham. The rich man also died and was buried. In Hades, where he was being tormented, he looked up and saw Abraham far away with Lazarus by his side. He called out, "Father Abraham, have mercy on me, and send Lazarus to dip the tip of his finger in water and cool my tongue; for I am in agony in these flames." But Abraham said, "Child, remember that during your lifetime you received your good things, and Lazarus in like manner evil things; but now he is comforted here, and you are in agony. Besides all this, between you and us a great chasm has been fixed, so that those who might want to pass from here to you cannot do so, and no one can cross from there to us." (Luke 16:19-26)

One thing we can learn from this parable is that we cannot give from beyond the grave. Dives stepped over Lazarus each day and apparently did not even notice him. He became aware of his lack of generosity in the next life, but by then it was too late.

Jesus teaches the same thing in the parable of the sheep and the goats (Matthew 25:32-46). When Jesus comes back in glory he will separate people into two groups, one comprising people who cared for those in need, and one comprising those who did not. Then the time for caring is over, and we will reap what we sowed. These parables must not be read as a call to works righteousness. Good works cannot save us. But our faith must find expression in our actions, and grace should inspire us to serve. If we live doxologically, with gratitude and thanksgiving for what we have been given, we will naturally give of our time, talents and treasures to those in need.

Perhaps the reality that our time to be generous is limited will prevent us from delay.

AN UNEXPECTED PHONE CALL

About a year after I helped the hungry young man in the opening story of this chapter, I received a call. "Pastor Smith?" a voice said. It was the young man I had helped. He went on to tell me that since the day I paid for his dinner, his life began to turn around. He found a job at a car wash and saved enough for an apartment. Then he found an even better job. His longtime girlfriend was able to come to the United States from Germany, and they were engaged. He offered to repay me for the meal, but I refused. He said, "All right, but please know that when I was in need, you helped me out. And I will always be grateful."

Though this story ended well, generosity does not always lead to this kind of result. Paul famously wrote, "Each of you must give as you have made up your mind, not reluctantly or under compulsion, for God loves a cheerful giver" (2 Corinthians 9:7). I want to be clear: I did not give cheerfully when I bought this man his dinner. While God loves giving with a glad heart, even our reluctant giving can be a blessing. I learned from this young man that even a small gift, given begrudgingly, can make a difference. In the end, the person who was helped the most that evening was me.

stewardship of resources

One of the principles of this chapter is that *frugality creates margin which enables generosity*. This is true in the five areas of stewardship (soul, body, time, talent, treasure). When we are frugal—not stingy but wise—we can then free up more resources in order to be generous. Since it is more difficult to find ways to be frugal or generous with soul and body (though they are important in the spiritual life), this week I would like you to experiment with being frugal, then generous, with your time, talent and treasure. Try to do all three exercises. (There is an additional fourth exercise that may be helpful to you where you are.) As always, though, pray about which and how many exercises you should do this week. And remember, a good rule of thumb is to ask, What is the most loving thing I can do in my situation?

BEING FRUGAL, THEN GENEROUS, WITH YOUR TIME
Being frugal. This week find ways to trim some of the activities in your life. This may be challenging: your schedule may be filled with work, family time and caring for others. But it may be possible to find ways to cut out or cut back a few activities. For example, the average American watches twenty-eight hours of television each week, and spends a few hours a day on the Internet. If this is true for you, perhaps you could try limiting your time in these activities by an hour

or two a day, freeing up time to invest in some activities you have been neglecting.

Being generous. If you have created some time margin, think of ways you can use that time to bless others. Maybe you could spend a little more time with a friend or family member you wish you had more time to be with. Offer to go for a walk or for coffee, or just hang out in your home, being present to them. You could also offer one of these hours to a shelter or soup kitchen, or any number of activities your church is sponsoring.

BEING FRUGAL, THEN GENEROUS, WITH YOUR TALENT

Being frugal. Many of us are overextended when it comes to our talents. I know people who are close to exhaustion because they have trouble saying no. As a consequence, they have little to give and feel put upon because they lack margin. This week try saying, "No, I am not able to do that right now." That will feel like a sin if you have been living with the narrative "Never say no to any request." But in truth you must find margin or you cannot be generous. You cannot help every friend, be on every committee or sing in every praise group. Find ways to get margin with your gifts so you can give freely when and where you are being led. This, of course, assumes that you will spend time in discernment.

Being generous. If you have found margin with your talents, then you are in a position to wait for God to use your gifts in a more balanced way. Take the posture of listening and discernment, and be open to letting God deploy your gifts in new ways.

BEING FRUGAL, THEN GENEROUS, WITH YOUR TREASURES

Being frugal. There are many ways to be more frugal with your financial resources, but perhaps the easiest is to not spend as much, or even any, on things that are not completely necessary. For example, for an extended time a friend of mine chose not to buy anything non-perishable (e.g., clothes, CDs, electronic gadgets, etc.). He still had to eat, of course, but he chose to forgo any new purchases for a while, and in so doing increased the money he had to give. Another way is to evaluate your purchases for a week and buy only that which is necessary. Small steps in frugality can create the financial margin needed in order to be generous.

Being generous. The same friend who stopped buying nonperishables was able to give money to two people who unexpectedly shared a financial need. They did not ask him for money, but after being made aware of their need he prayed about it and then gave money to help them out. Had he not been frugal, he could not have been generous.

There are many other ways you will discover to be frugal with your time, talents and treasures. As a result, God will give you opportunities to be generous that you might not have been able to respond to before.

YOUR GENEROUS COMMUNITY

In this chapter I wrote about the service of being served and mentioned people in my life who are generous with their love, support, protection, wisdom and encouragement. A helpful exercise may be for you to write a paragraph or two like the one I wrote, naming specific people in your life and the way they bless you. This could be used to deepen your gratitude to God. It may also create a desire in you to write a note, a card or an email to the people mentioned in your paragraph, thanking them for the blessing they are in your life.

eight

The worshiping community

One of the tasks of a first-year associate pastor, I learned quickly, is doing the tasks that need to be done but no one wants to do. In my first church appointment after seminary I found myself in that position. The senior pastor was concerned that our membership roll was much higher than our Sunday attendance numbers, which meant that a lot of people were considered members of the church even though they had not attended in a long time. I was assigned the task of calling on each "member" who had not worshiped in the church for three or more years. I took the membership roll, went to my office and began making phone calls. Some of the people had moved away; others had died. I asked if I could visit those who were still in town. Out of one hundred calls, only four showed any interest in a visit from me. Out of those four, two families returned to the church, and one decided to join another church.

The fourth call affected me the most: a divorced mother of grown children. She said little in our brief conversation but said she would love to have me over for tea. She took the initiative by asking me a lot of questions about my personal spiritual life. Eventually I asked her similar questions, and she became very animated. "Well, my rela-

tionship with God is everything to me. I spend an hour each morning in meditation and prayer, and an hour before bed doing the same.
Would you like to see where I pray?" she asked. She took me to
a special room in her home. The walls were covered in religious
imagery—crosses, icons and paintings of religious figures. In the
corner was a kind of altar or shrine with a kneeling bench. Beaming,
she said, "This is where I connect to God."

We resumed our conversation back in the living room over a second cup of tea. Eventually I asked, "I was wondering, will we be seeing you in worship one of these Sundays?" She replied quickly, "Oh
no, church is not for me. I have all I need here in my prayer room. I
get too discouraged by corporate worship. I am fine. But thank you
for inviting me. I suppose you should take me off of the membership
roll." I stammered for a moment, searching for something wise to
say, but all I could think of was, "Are you sure you don't want to
come back?" Again she responded politely, "No thank you, Reverend.
As I said, I have all I need right here. But thank you for coming and
visiting with me. I liked hearing about your own journey into God."

> Have you ever encountered someone who refused to worship corporately? What did you say to them then? What would you say to them now?

As I drove back to the church I
was profoundly discouraged. I had spent years training for ministry in
the local church, and yet I had no response when a person told me that
she had no need for the church, that she was just fine without it. I
wondered, *Could she be right? Can a Christian live without a worshiping
community?* I had no answer because I had some false narratives of my
own concerning the church and corporate worship.

FALSE AND TRUE NARRATIVES ABOUT WORSHIP

The woman who worshiped privately in her home impressed me. She was dedicated, she was engaged, and the way she worshiped God seemed to have a positive impact on her life. As an introverted contemplative I completely understood how that kind of worship could be meaningful and transforming. My own experience affirmed this. For many years I began each morning with an hour or more of solitude, prayer, silence, Bible reading and journaling—complete with candles. These were rich hours for me, and they deepened my relationship with God. I also understood her reluctance to take part in corporate worship. In church I often found it distracting and difficult to focus on God. To this day I would affirm her private practice of daily worship. However, I would also encourage her to engage in public worship with a community of believers. Let me explain why.

She, like me for many years, was living by an incomplete narrative.

False narrative: Worship is a personal matter meant to inspire the individual. For her, worship is merely private, and its aim is to create an emotional sensation. Everything she needs is found in her solitary room. While we can (and should) worship privately, and we can (and should) experience inspiration, that is not the primary reason for corporate worship; it is not about individual inspiration but rather the transformation of the person *within*, *by* and *for* the community.

People say, "I go to church to get inspired." I think this *can* be a noble, even godly, desire. We are hungering for a deeper life with God, and our time in worship can be a way to make us feel connected. Looking forward to that is no sin. But I am concerned when this personal, individual need eclipses the need to take part in something bigger than the individual, which may or may not feel good to us. While church need not be boring, it is also not designed merely to give us good feelings. Too often the church tries to compete with secular forms of entertainment, and too often this leads to pale imitations (e.g., top ten lists from the pulpit). While inspiration is a by-product of worship, it is not the central aim of worship.

True narrative: Worship is a communal activity meant to instruct a people. From our roots in Judaism to the earliest expression in the *ecclesia* of Christ, worship has always been a corporate activity. We worship because *we* are a peculiar people whose roots are in the future. We tell our stories, learn our language and find our life in the presence of other Christ-followers. We go to church not to be entertained but to be trained. The church is the only place where we hear the true story of who God is, who we are and what our lives are all about.

In thinking back to chapter seven, do you see how you bless others and how others bless you? how corporately you function as a body for the building up of one another? Share your thoughts with your community.

Another false narrative is the opposite of the first, but it can be equally destructive.

False narrative: Worship is an obligation we owe to God. A common narrative is that we are obliged to worship God. It is used to motivate people to go to church. In truth, God does not need our worship. God is perfectly fine without it, but we need to worship. When we worship we are aligned with the truth, and our souls function well when immersed in the truth.

True narrative: Worship is an invitation given by God. Far from an *obligation*, worship is an *invitation* from a gracious God. Worship is our response to what God has done and is doing. Worship is an invitation from a gracious God who bids us to come and enjoy his beauty and goodness. The psalmist writes,

> For a day in your courts is better
>   than a thousand elsewhere.
> I would rather be a doorkeeper in the house of my God
>   than live in the tents of wickedness. (Psalm 84:10)

Worship, including the practices that make it up, is a powerful means of forming God's people through its unique language and practices.

Worship is a gift, a blessing and something we long for once we have truly experienced it. Alfred North Whitehead famously said, "Religion is what an individual does with his solitariness." I suppose that is my chief problem with this false narrative: it is a *religious* practice. Christianity is not a religion but the formation of a people through the gospel—the good news that God in Christ has reconciled the world. Religion is the human search for God; Christianity is God's search for humans. We do not worship so much as we respond. "Through Christ in the Spirit we respond to the Father's love. This is the ground-pattern of Christian worship."

LOOKING BEYOND AESTHETICS

The day I visited the woman who worshiped privately was painful because I did not know how to respond to her. It was years later that I read the words of C. S. Lewis, who provided an excellent answer. To a friend he wrote:

> When I first became a Christian, about fourteen years ago, I thought that I could do it on my own, by retiring to my rooms and reading theology, and I wouldn't go to churches and Gospel Halls; . . . I disliked very much their hymns, which I considered fifth-rate poems set to sixth-rate music. But as I went on I saw the great merit of it. I came up against different people of quite different outlooks and different education, and then gradually my conceit just began peeling off. I realized that the hymns (which were just sixth-rate music) were, nonetheless, being sung with devotion and benefit by an old saint in elastic boots in the opposite pew, and then you realize that you aren't fit to clean those boots. It gets you out of your solitary conceit.

We can learn much from Lewis's insights. First, Lewis thought he could live the Christian life by reading theology books alone in his room. He later learned this does not suffice.

Second, the music paled in comparison to the great composers. Later, though, Lewis was able to penetrate beneath the surface and into the heart of the worshiper, who is not moved by the aesthetic performance but by the pulsing love of God. When he looked at the "old saint in elastic boots," who at one time he judged as unsophisticated, he saw someone he was not worthy of, for this old saint's passion and devotion to God connect him or her to the sacred.

> What do you connect to from your own experience in Lewis's perspective on the church?

Solitary conceit, Lewis says, kept him from the gathered people of God. It was *solitary* because he thought he could do it alone, and *conceit* because he thought Christian worship not worthy of his appreciation. But when God stepped in and taught him a new narrative, Lewis was able to see the invaluable worth of corporate worship. We would do well to remember this. We need each other, despite our differences. Worship is not about the quality of the performance but the heart of those who worship. Worship is not about "individual fulfillment" but the "constitution of a people."

WORSHIP CAN BE BORING

A people group is missing in our churches. They are a very specific group, at least in terms of age. They are the eighteen- to twenty-nine-year-olds. Some church experts call these "the missing years." Once young people turn eighteen, they typically stop going to church. We see them return, like the swallows of Capistrano, twelve years later, often because they are married and have had their first child, and church seems like the right thing to do. But why do they leave at eighteen? As the parent of a seventeen-year-old who has grown up in the church, I thought it would be good for me to find out what he thinks about church worship. We sat down one Saturday afternoon and had a discussion about his likes and dislikes of Sunday worship.

"What do you like about church, Jake?" I asked.

"The sermons sometimes are my favorite part," he answered. "Not all of them, just the ones I can relate to, the encouraging ones."

"What is your least favorite part?" I followed up by asking.

"I don't like singing. Well, I like listening to people sing, but not singing out loud with others. It doesn't seem important."

"All singing?"

"No, I do like hymns. I just have a hard time relating God to a rock band—I can't see Jesus playing lead guitar. I liked those times we went to the Orthodox service—the chanting sounded cool. But the service was too long, and I didn't like standing the whole time. I'm not a big stander," he answered.

"What other parts of worship do you enjoy, or get something out of?" I asked.

"I like praying. But sometimes the pastors pray too long. I also like hearing the Bible read, or reading it out loud together. I also like when we say the Apostles' Creed, because we learned it together," he said.

"What about the things we do as a group, like baptizing people or taking Communion?"

"Seeing someone get baptized is fine. I like that. I also like Communion a lot—but I wish we had real bread rather than wafers. They taste kind of bad."

"You yourself were baptized in the same church we still attend. You have grown up with this community. What do you think of when you think about the people?" I asked.

"Our church has grown a lot,

Reflectively journal on what you like about worshiping in your community. What draws you closer? What would you prefer to change? What can you learn from those things you'd change?

so I don't know everyone, but seeing people who know me, who say, 'Jacob, I remember you when you were five years old running down the aisle' is kind of nice. I like the older people; they are the nicest."

I learned a lot in this short conversation. I was surprised to hear Jake likes hymns, and even more surprised he does not like the band. In my generation we rejected the hymns and loved having electric guitars in worship. Perhaps something is shifting, or maybe it is just him. I found it interesting that Jake enjoys the parts that are the least like the world he normally lives in. No one says the creeds, preaches about Jesus or partakes of Communion in day-to-day life outside of the church. I will hang on to this should he, like so many, take a twelve-year sabbatical from corporate worship.

I can hear some people saying, "You should *make* him go to church, even when he is eighteen." That goes against my entire understanding of the nature of the kingdom of God and of the human heart. I will trust in the goodness of God, who has made himself known to Jake through the years. Those sermons did not fall on bad soil. Those times of taking Communion, of listening to the Bible, of praying with people will not go to waste. Instead of making him stay connected to church, I might try to get him to read the following section of this chapter. Instead of making people feel guilty about not going to church, I would rather try to make people excited about the opportunity, which can only happen when we really understand what worship is all about.

WORSHIP IS WORTH IT

Let's take a closer look at the practices of worship, which will help us overcome the false narratives of self-fulfillment or divine obligation, and move us to long to be in the house of God.

The earliest Christians came from Jewish backgrounds. They modified the worship practices of Judaism in light of their newfound faith. Over the centuries Christian worship has been shaped into a cohesive form. Though some people believe we should imitate the practices of the early Christians, I believe that the shaping of worship through the centuries is a sign of God's movement among his people.

The New Testament does not offer a set form of worship to be followed by all Christians for all ages. There is great freedom when it comes to forms of worship. In fact, through the centuries worship styles and practices have been modified to help connect the truths of the faith to new generations. Chants became hymns, and hymns became praise choruses, for example.

Though the form of worship is not the main focus, this does not mean form is unimportant. Form matters. There are basic elements of Christian worship that have been found useful in the development of our relationship with God and others. Though not all Christian groups engage in all of these elements of worship, many groups use some or all of these practices consistently in their gatherings. We will look at each of these briefly in order to explain how they form us spiritually. I will write the following as if I were writing to my son to explain why worship is worth it.

A LETTER TO MY SON ON WHAT IS GREAT ABOUT WORSHIP

Dear Jacob,

Even though you grew up going to church each Sunday, there will come a day when *you* will choose whether to go to church. Your mother and I will not make you go, and we will try hard not to make you feel guilty if you choose not to. But I would like you to consider thinking a little bit about what we do in worship, things that I believe you will need to live a full and joyful life. I know that church can be as boring as watching paint dry, and I have often cringed when someone implies that heaven will be an unending worship service. God forbid. But I do believe that our gathered worship is special, sacred and necessary. Let me explain why by talking about the common elements of Christian worship.

Greeting. One of the first things we do when we gather is greet one another. The early Christians did this with a "holy kiss," but that was dropped for obvious reasons. What is important about greeting is simply acknowledging each other's presence. We all hunger to know and be known; as the old TV show *Cheers* said, we all want to go to a place where everybody knows our name. The world can be pretty cold and ruthless. It is a dog-eat-dog world outside of the kingdom of God. So it feels great to go to a place that seems to really want you—the smiling guy at the door, the nice lady who offers you coffee. No matter what state or country you are in, if you go to Christian worship, someone will greet you, and you will feel as if you are home. Which, of course, you are.

Confession and forgiveness. Despite your best effort, you will fail to lead a perfect life, and in time, Jake, you will blow it and will need a place to deal with your feelings. If we are honest with God and ourselves, we need a time and a place to confess our failure. Some communities do this formally, using written prayers led by a pastor or said in unison: "Most merciful God, we confess that we have sinned against you in thought, word, and deed, by what we have done, and by what we have left undone." This practice is then followed by a leader who offers words of assurance: "Hear the good news: Christ died for us while we were yet sinners; that proves God's love toward us. In the name of Jesus Christ, we are forgiven! Amen!" Some groups do this informally, allowing a time of silent reflection. Either way, the practice helps keep us honest, shapes our desire to walk in holiness and allows another apprentice to speak words of comfort. Sin does not get the last word; forgiveness is the last word. Forgiveness is something you will desperately need to experience.

Creeds, commandments and the Lord's Prayer. The early Christians developed creeds (from the Latin *credo,* meaning, "This I believe") as a way of explaining the metanarrative in a shortened form. From the Apostles' Creed to the Nicene Creed, Christ-followers have recited these highly charged words as a means of keeping their beliefs ever before them, and as a way of denying heretical beliefs. The reciting of the creeds establishes us as Christians and connects us to the body of Christ through the ages. Though not all communities recite the creeds, for many it is a way to tell the story of our faith in a way that all can understand it. The Lord's Prayer and the Ten Commandments can also be used in this way.

You learned these when you were young. We placed the Ten Commandments, the Lord's Prayer and the Apostles' Creed above your bed. You have kept them there ever since then, which impressed me. Each night when you were young we would say them together and talk about their meaning. You memorized the Ten Commandments first. We would talk about what it means to have other gods before God, what the sabbath is all about and why we should not bear false witness. We did the same with the Lord's Prayer and the Apostles' Creed. The idea certainly was not mine! These are the basis of the Christian catechism (Protestant and Catholic) dating back hundreds of years. They are statements that the church is founded on. In a world that will tell you right and wrong are subjective, and that belief is only a personal matter, they offer solid answers.

Scripture and sermon. Your life is a story. Worshiping communities read the Bible in worship and preach sermons as a means of telling our story, which is your story, the story into which you were baptized. Our whole church pledged to raise you in the Christian faith, the story that binds us all together.

Some communities hear the Word in the context of the sermon, which can serve as an explanation and application of the text. The Bible is our common text; it unites us. Preaching, particularly when it springs from the Scriptures, proclaims the great truths of our faith and is a means of grace whereby God comforts or convicts—and sometimes elevates—his people.

In my life I have witnessed several occasions when a preacher became infused with the power of the Spirit in such a way that all I could do was sit in awe. My friend and colleague Bill Vaswig is the finest preacher I have ever heard. There have been times when he has lifted my heart and mind to places I have only dreamed of. No wonder the Bible proclaims, "How beautiful are the feet of those who bring good news!" (Romans 10:15; Isaiah 52:7).

I hope you remember to give thanks for those in our midst who come with beautiful feet. There is no other place on earth that can tell you your story.

Communion or the Lord's Supper. We read in Acts that the first Christians shared a meal when they gathered together: "They devoted themselves to the apostles' teaching and fellowship, to the breaking of bread and the prayers" (Acts 2:42). By the time Paul had established churches among the Gentiles, what we know as the Lord's Supper was a standard part of worship (1 Corinthians 11:23-26). The meal became a reminder of the death of Jesus and all of its blessed implications. In fact, *the act of Communion symbolizes all that I love about Christian community.*

First, the meal reminded them that they were an *eternal community* because of their participation in the eternal Christ (1

Corinthians 10:16). The bread and the cup became a way to "set [their] minds on things that are above" because they too had died, and their life was now hidden with Christ in God (Colossians 3:1-4). The miracle of co-crucifixion and co-resurrection was experienced in the bread and the cup—representing the body and blood of Jesus.

Second, the people practiced being an *unselfish* and *generous community*. The Lord's Supper reminded them to make sure everyone had enough to eat and drink. When they failed to do this (some ate and drank too much) Paul scolded them (1 Corinthians 11:20-22, 33-34). This, by the way, is what Paul meant by taking Communion in an "unworthy manner" (1 Corinthians 11:27), and not, as many suppose, taking the Lord's Supper with unconfessed sin.

Third, the meal demonstrated that they were a *unified community*. Paul used the metaphor of the loaf to remind them that they were one body: "Because there is one loaf, we, who are many, are one body, for we all partake of the one loaf" (1 Corinthians 10:17 NIV). Though they were diverse (Jew and Gentile, male and female, slave and free) they were one in Christ, symbolized by the one loaf of which they all partook. The common bread and common cup reminded them of their common life.

Fourth, the cup reminded them that they were a *reconciling community*. Jesus said, "This is my blood of the covenant, which is poured out for many for the forgiveness of sins" (Matthew 26:28). The meal was a reminder of their forgiveness, making it both possible and necessary to forgive one another. Having Christ dwell in them through this meal also reminded them that they were a *holy community*, set apart to do good works. A simple meal of bread and wine told their story and reminded them of who they were and who they were called to be. Ordinary

elements such as bread and wine—which are created by God—
are lifted up into something new.

There is a lot of debate, even fighting and schism, over what
the bread and the cup actually are or symbolize. It is ironic that
the meal that was meant to unite so often has divided us. No
matter where you end up worshiping, I hope you grow to appreciate this ancient Christian practice.

Singing. I know that singing is not your favorite part of worship, but it is important. In addition to the breaking of bread,
the early Christians also sang:

> Let the word of Christ dwell in you richly; teach and ad-
> monish one another in all wisdom; and with gratitude in
> your hearts sing psalms, hymns, and spiritual songs to
> God. (Colossians 3:16)

> Sing psalms and hymns and spiritual songs among your-
> selves, singing and making melody to the Lord in your
> hearts. (Ephesians 5:19)

Throughout the history of the church, singing has been an
important and life-giving practice. Through song we tell our
story, offer praise and experience the joy that can only come
through music. God designed us in such a way that sound and
rhythm inspire and motivate us. Music touches us at an emotional and bodily level, and when it is used to offer praise to God,
it connects us to the Trinity and each other in ways that teaching
and preaching cannot. Singing involves our whole bodies—
stomachs, tongues, lungs and even hands as we clap or raise our
hands in the air. In this sense worship is a holistic practice.

Silence. We live in a noisy world, and if your soul is going
to experience rest or make a connection with God, you will
need some spaces for silence. Many churches allow silence to

live and breathe, which is something I love. We can only sense the leading of the Spirit when we are still. We get so little silence in our world, and we desperately need it for the well-being of our souls. Silence in worship is another sign of peculiarity. Silence, or at least pausing for a few moments of reflection, is the only way we can let the Word of God sink into our hearts and minds. I hope you one day find a church that values silence.

Offering gifts. When you were little, we let you put the family offering envelope, and sometimes your own change, into the offering plate. Some people think money has no place in worship. But it does. Giving is itself an act of worship. This is not a way of paying for admission but of offering our gifts to God. The world tells us to look out for ourselves. Offering our gifts helps us let go of the need to store up treasures for ourselves. I hope you learn the joy of giving, and the truth that what we give to advance the work of the kingdom is never lost.

Benediction or sending forth. Often the final act of worship is an official sending forth. It is often called a *benediction*. The pastor or leader usually offers parting words that encourage the congregation to go forth with the blessing of God. "The Lord bless you and keep you, the Lord make his face to shine upon you and be gracious to you; the Lord turn his face toward you and give you peace," for example. This reminds us that we are to be light to a darkened world. As we were summoned to worship, now we are sent into the world.

As a father whose life has been transformed by Jesus, there is nothing more I want for you. I want it more than I want you to have success or fame. I would love to hear one day, "Hey, Dad, I got this great job, and I really love it. They pay me well." But I would love even more to hear you say, "Hey, Dad, I found this great church. The people are loving, and the sermons challenge and inspire me. Worship is a source of strength for me, and it is shaping my entire life. Thanks for raising me in church." Oh what a happy day that will be.

A GLIMPSE OF ETERNITY IN THE ORDINARY

In his masterful novel *Jayber Crow*, Wendell Berry tells the story of a man who renounces his call to become a minister and instead becomes a barber. Still, Jayber never abandons his love for the church. One day, while sweeping the empty church he has grown up in, he has a dream that helps him see the eternal dimension of the church as it worships. Alexander Schmemann said worship is the epiphany of the world. In the eyes of Jayber Crow, the church in all of its earthy, human, broken and prideful forms was seen from the perspective of eternity.

One day when I went up there to work, sleepiness overcame me and I lay down on the floor behind the back pew to take a nap. Waking or sleeping (I couldn't tell which), I saw all the people gathered there who had ever been there. I saw them as I had seen them from the back pew, where I sat with Uncle Othy (who would not come any farther) while Aunt Cordie sang in the choir, and I saw them as I had seen them (from the back pew) on the Sunday before. I saw them in all the times past and to come, all somehow there in their own time and in all time and in no time: the cheerfully working and singing women, the men quiet or reluctant or shy, the weary, the troubled in spirit, the sick, the lame, the desperate, the dying, the little children tucked in the pews beside their elders, the young married couples full of visions, the old men with their dreams, the parents of their proud children, the grandparents with tears in their eyes, the pairs of young lovers attentive only to each other on the edge of the world, the grieving widows and widowers, the mothers and fathers of children newly dead, the proud, the humble, the attentive, the distracted—I saw them all. I saw the creases crisscrossed in the backs of men's necks, their work-thickened hands, the Sunday dresses faded with washing. They were just there. They said nothing, and I said nothing. I seemed to love them all with a love that was mine merely because it included me. When I came to myself again, my face was wet with tears.

I love this story because it reminds me that the church is both earthy (reluctant, troubled, distracted people) and yet eternal. I started this chapter by asking, Can we live the Christian life without a worshiping community? I would answer, Yes, it is possible—all things are possible with God. But the better question is, Why would we even want to try?

worship

The exercise for this week is to go to church with what Richard Foster calls "holy expectancy." For many of us, attending church is fraught with frustration and distraction: "We are running late—hurry up!" or "Oh no, someone is sitting in my seat" or "I can't believe she wore that!" or "The sermon was way too long today." In this chapter I have tried to focus on the right narratives about worship: it is an invitation (not an obligation) and is not about meeting my needs as much as shaping my soul. We also looked at some of the basic elements of worship, focusing on their meaning and impact.

For this reason, I would like you to make your corporate worship more meaningful by engaging in a few acts of preparation. The following are some guidelines, not laws, that may be helpful as you seek to experience the wonder of worship.

ENGAGING IN MEANINGFUL WORSHIP

1. Prepare through margin. Simply getting to worship with the right attitude is a challenge for many of us. The culprit is not our lack of desire but our lack of temporal margin. The proper attitude for worship cannot be cultivated in the ten seconds we spend walking through the narthex. We must prepare for worship long before that. One way is to go to bed early on the evening before worship. This will allow us to awaken earlier, which will create some margin in terms of time. We need a few hours to eat and dress and prepare our hearts for worship. *Time* margin is thus necessary in order to create *heart* margin.

2. Arrive early. A simple but effective way for me to be more attentive in worship is to come well before the service begins in order to become fully present. Richard Foster offers this advice: "Enter the service ten minutes early. Lift your heart in adoration to the King of glory." This has helped me appreciate worship and has reduced the distractions that often happen when I arrive late.

3. Come with holy expectancy. As previously noted, Foster encourages a sense of holy expectancy among worshipers. This can be done by a simple prayer: "Spirit, speak to me. Jesus, teach me. Father, let me experience your love and power." I believe this is a prayer God loves to answer. And it is a prayer that awakens our desire.

4. Focus on one aspect of worship this week. There are many acts within a worship service (e.g., sermon, Bible reading, singing, Communion). This week focus on one particular element of worship. For example, if you choose singing, pay attention to your body, to the sounds and to the words being sung. Reflect on its meaning—why do we sing? What is happening to us as a community as we sing? You can pick a different aspect each week. If you do this each week, over the course of a few months you will have reflected on nearly every aspect of worship, thus enabling an entire worship service to become an act of doxology.

5. Apply one thing. Worship transforms us and leads us into new ways of living. Foster wisely writes, "Just as worship begins in holy expectancy it ends in holy obedience." This week pay attention to what God might be asking you to *do*. Is there someone you need to speak with? A change you need to make? A new practice you need to make as you walk with God? Keep it simple and try to discern what *one* thing God may be asking of you, and then labor to put it into practice this week.

nine

writing a soul-training plan

Sometimes the end is just the beginning. I know from experience that when I come to the end of a Bible study, a Sunday school class or a retreat that has been helpful to me, I often feel a bit lost. What will I do now? How will I possibly be able to continue the good things God seems to be working in me? Having come to the end of this series, some readers will be asking, What do I do now? The first answer is, Be with God in all of the ways you can, and continue letting the teachings of Jesus shape your mind.

There is one final exercise that I recommend, which is to create a plan for continued growth developed by you and God, and perhaps others. It is not written in stone but is for your life right now, which will likely change over time.

I have found that having a strategy, as well as a community to support me, to be extremely helpful. And yet it is something very few Christians practice. Why? There are two false narratives that inhibit people from creating a plan and joining with others: (1) I don't need a plan, and (2) I can do it on my own.

For some reason we think that our life with God does not require effort or planning; it will just happen. Unfortunately, it never does. Regarding the first false narrative, if you fail to plan *you are planning to fail*. Nothing in life happens without planning, without a strategy. If you want to plant a garden or lose weight or learn how to speak Spanish, you need a plan. The same is true for spiritual formation.

Regarding the second narrative, *you cannot do it on your own*, nor are you expected to try. We are not designed to live in isolation. Other people can offer us support, encouragement, wisdom and discernment. The Christian life is meant to be lived in community, with people who are intentionally with you, who support you and will do what they can to help nurture your faith. There are many people who are willing to walk with you. Perhaps you already have such a group. If not, seek the help of a local church or try going online to The Apprentice Series website (www.apprenticeofjesus.org). You may be able to find an apprentice group in your area or a church that uses this curriculum and may already have "Apprentices for Life" groups you can join.

How can you continue on this path? I would encourage you to do two things: first, establish a plan to keep studying Jesus' core narratives and keep practicing the spiritual exercises that go with them. Second, find others who will walk with you in this endeavor, holding you accountable in a loving way and encouraging you to keep going.

AN ANCIENT PRACTICE
Early Christian communities used the word *rule* to describe their strategy for growth. The idea of a rule comes from the Latin word *regula*, which refers to a rule or covenant that states your intentions. The first *regula* was an early Christian document called the *Didache*, probably written in the early second century. It detailed a way of life for the early Christians. Another rule was written by Saint Augustine in the fifth century. The most popular and enduring *regula* was written by Saint Benedict in the sixth century. Many other rules have been written for Christian communities through the ages, both Catholic and Protestant. The Methodist movement contained rules

for the societies, classes and bands, which laid out the plans and expectations of those who called themselves Methodists. The word *rule* can seem legalistic and confining, so I have found the words *plan* and *strategy* to be more helpful.

What does a strategy do for people? It is a balanced and wholesome pattern that helps define how we want to live. It is a constant reminder of how we would like to live. It can help us to go beyond merely good intentions and into action. It is not a set of laws or an oppressive, guilt-inducing document that will make life miserable.

Unlike the rules of Saints Augustine or Benedict, I am not recommending a standard rule for every member of an apprentice group. Instead I will offer some guidelines for helping you create your own balanced program for living as an apprentice of Jesus. Then I suggest you share your plan with a group—if possible a group of people who have been through the series. (They will have a shared vocabulary and will have engaged in the same exercises.) Please note that the strategy I am suggesting is *not* a set of laws but a life rhythm. Though not a rigid set of exercises, neither is a rule mere suggestions we can choose to ignore—at least not if our desire is to continue to grow.

1. WRITING A SOUL-TRAINING PLAN— A *REGULA* FOR LIFE

When asked what the greatest commandment is, Jesus answered:

> "You shall love the Lord your God with all your heart, and with all your soul, and with all your mind." This is the greatest and first commandment. And a second is like it: "You shall love your neighbor as yourself." On these two commandments hang all the law and the prophets. (Matthew 22:37-40)

The first and greatest commandment is that we love God with all that we are: heart and soul and mind. The second commandment is that we love our neighbor as we love ourselves. This implies that we ought to love ourselves. *Love*, as defined in this series, is "to will the good of another." We are to labor to care for ourselves and for one another.

"Love God and take care of yourself and each other" might be a summation of the passage. If this is our greatest task, then we need a plan, a strategy, to ensure that we are doing it as best we can. A helpful way to do this is to practice ways that allow us to do all three. The soul-training exercises at the end of each chapter of the books in The Apprentice Series can be divided into these three areas: ways we increase our love for God, ways we take care of ourselves and ways we work for the good of others. Below are the thirty-three soul-training exercises that have been recommended in this series, divided under the three headings of God, self and others.

God
- Silence and Awareness of Creation
- Counting Your Blessings
- Praying Psalm 23
- *Lectio Divina*
- Reading the Gospel of John
- Solitude
- Writing a Letter to God
- Living One Day Devotionally
- Reading a Devotional Classic
- Reading the Bible During Free Times
- Two Hours with God
- Worship

Self
- Sleep
- Silence

- Margin
- Slowing Down
- Play
- Keeping the Sabbath
- Media Fast
- Nonspeaking
- Finding an Accountability Friend
- Forgiveness Exercises

Others

- Hospitality
- Praying for the Success of Competitors
- Secret Service
- Deaccumulation
- Prayer
- A Day Without Gossip
- Four Acts of Peculiarity
- Sharing Your faith
- Treasuring Our Treasures
- Loving Those We Disagree With
- Stewardship of Resources

Look over the list and make mental notes of your experiences with the exercises. You may even want to put stars by some of them, or rate them on a scale of one to ten in terms of how they affected you.

Step 1: Picking from the list. The first step in writing your plan is to pick several (five to ten) soul-training exercises from the preceding lists that were especially transforming for you. Do not just pick those you liked the most; pick the ones that will most help you grow in your life with God. For example, doing a forty-eight-hour media fast may not have been pleasant, but it may have been very beneficial. Try to narrow your list to around six or seven exercises. This will be a good place to start. One of the key things about writing a rule is to start with small, achievable goals. A common mistake is when people want to do too much and end up failing to keep their plan. I suggest that you try to include at least two exercises from each of the three categories.

Step 2: Adding practices not on the list. The exercises listed are not the only ways people can nurture their life with God. There are countless other spiritual exercises that people find meaningful. For example, I like to read the sermons of John Wesley, Martin Luther and George MacDonald because they inspire me and increase my love and devotion to God. I also enjoy using the daily devotional *The Upper Room.*

In addition to spiritual exercises there are also other nurturing practices that you may engage in from time to time. Usually these fall under the second category, self-care. I really enjoy riding horses, walking my dog and reading old novels. I have friends who love to go sailing or to knit. One student once told me he loves watching old movies. Come up with a few things that you find fulfilling but you don't usually get around to doing. They may not seem "spiritual," but if they affect your well-being they are spiritual.

With these three to five additional practices added to your original list from The Apprentice Series, your list should include ten to twelve practices that you believe will help increase your love for God, self and neighbor.

Step 3: Timing and frequency. The next step is to determine how often and how long you will practice these exercises. For example, let's say you chose Bible reading as a helpful exercise. Think about how often you would like to read the Bible each week: perhaps daily or maybe two to three times a week. Then determine how long (fifteen minutes or a half hour?) or how much of the Bible (one, two or five chapters?) you want to read. Another example: will you ride your horse every week or once a month? Think about how much you need to engage in these exercises in order to get the most benefit, without overdoing it, getting frustrated and quitting.

Step 4: Creating a plan with balance and moderation. There are two criteria I would like you to think about as you look at your list. First, is the rule you have created balanced, that is, are there the right number of exercises in each of the three areas (God, self, others)? Second, is the rule attainable? It must be *balanced* if you are to grow, and it must *attainable* if you are to sustain it. You may not be able to answer this question right away. The first rule I wrote was neither balanced nor attainable. I put too many exercises on the list, with too much focus on exercises that developed my relationship with God. The frequency was also too high. I should have known I would fail when I wrote "three hours of time alone with God each day." This is nearly impossible in terms of my daily routine, and it is more than I needed in that area of my life. It is hard to know how you will do before actually trying it, but having others examine your rule to offer their guidance can help.

Figure 9.1 is an example of a rule written by my friend and fellow apprentice Jennifer Hinz. It is a good example of balance and moderation in caring for God, herself and others.

Jennifer's plan is excellent. She is a naturally giving person, so it was good to see that she included sewing (something that nourishes her soul) and margin. Jennifer was able to keep her *regula* for a long time because it was life-giving and challenging without being too demanding.

Figure 9.2 is the rule of my colleague Matt Johnson. Matt, as you will probably guess by looking at his plan, is a contemplative person who enjoys and benefits greatly from his times with God.

As you can see, Matt's rule contains several times for private prayer and solitude. His *regula* includes spending fifteen minutes a day practicing God's presence, a full hour of prayer on Monday morning, *lectio*

☐ count my blessings every Sunday before I go to sleep

☐ sew three times a month

☐ pray through Psalm 23 every morning

☐ take a drive every Sunday with my family to get ice cream

☐ give myself margin every weekend

☐ have dinner with friends two times a month

☐ pray for competitors every night before falling asleep

☐ go on a walk with my family once a week

☐ hospitality—serve others twice a month

☐ invite family and friends to our home for dinner
   twice a month

Figure 9.1. Jennifer's plan for life

divina twice a week and one hour of holy leisure three times a month. Those are very powerful spiritual exercises, but they are also very challenging for most people, who are not used to so much solitude.

Though his plan is weighted toward nurturing his relationship with God, I probably would not tell Matt to cut back on these practices because I know how much he benefits from them. I think he finds balance in that his *regula* includes enough self-care (gardening, guitar playing, dates with his wife and spiritual direction) as well as service to others (doing dishes daily, three acts of service a week). One of the best things Matt has going for him is that he works each month with a spiritual director, who is able to help him discern how his plan is beneficial and, if necessary, how to modify it.

2. ALLOWING OTHERS TO SHAPE YOUR PLAN
I have found it very helpful to have other apprentices look at my

☐ doing dishes two times each day for fifteen minutes
(a.m. and p.m.)

☐ practicing God's presence daily—6:45-7:00 a.m.

☐ gardening/working outside three times per week for thirty
minutes—Monday, Tuesday and Thursday—7:00-7:30 a.m.

☐ guitar playing four times per week for twenty minutes—
Monday through Thursday—9:20-9:40 a.m.

☐ contemplative/intercessory prayer once each week on
Monday morning

☐ *lectio divina* two times per week on Tuesday and Thursday

☐ solitude once each week for two hours on
Wednesday—7:20-9:20 a.m.

☐ welcoming prayer—review practice once each week on
Thursday—8:30 a.m.

☐ go out with Catherine once each week—one hour on
Thursday night

☐ sabbath three times per month Friday into Saturday

☐ service—three acts of service each week (hard to measure)

☐ spiritual direction once each month as scheduled

Figure 9.2. Matt's plan

regula and offer their input, especially in terms of balance and attainability. We are not always objective, and others may be able to see an area we have missed. One time I looked at the plan of a person in my group and immediately saw that it was imbalanced. It had two exercises that nurtured his life with God, no self-care exercises and ten aimed at helping others. This friend is a very giving, loving person who lives to serve. But I was able to point out the imbalance, which he could not see. This is a form of spiritual direction. We are allowing others to peer into our practices and offer their perspective, which is a great gift.

An alternative is to bring all of your plans together and write a common plan that everyone agrees to follow for a time. A friend of mine did this with a group of eight apprentices who had gone through the series together. When they finished the series, they took a month off to write their own rules. Then they came together and shared what each had written. Together they came up with a single rule with several exercises to be done each month that all of them agreed to practice (see fig. 9.3). Their group met every two weeks to share how they were doing. By email they also shared how they were doing, what was working and where they were struggling. This became a way to offer some tips they discovered along the way.

Notice the exercises they agreed on, as well as the frequency they chose to do them. The sabbath, for example, was important to nearly

☐ observe a sabbath on the third Sunday of the month

☐ read the Gospel of John in one sitting during the month

☐ daily reading of the Sermon on the Mount—approximately fifteen minutes a day during the workweek

☐ ten to twenty minutes of silence each day

☐ slow down: specifically drive the speed limit and be aware of God's presence; bless each driver that passes by

☐ at least once a week intentionally build up a new or current relationship by writing a note, sending an email or making a call

☐ lift each other up in daily prayer

Figure 9.3. A group rule

all of them, but they also knew that it can be hard for everyone to keep a sabbath every week. So they decided to all have a sabbath time together on the third Sunday of each month. This allowed them to help prepare each other for that day, as well as share ideas that worked for them. In reality, it turned out to be difficult for them to keep it on the same day.

Their group *regula* is attainable for the most part, but the practice of reading the Sermon on the Mount *daily* was a challenge because of their schedules. Some found it easy, especially those who had time on their lunch break, to sit down and read. They were surprised by how much impact other activities on the list had. For example, driving the speed limit (which is the *law*) had a big effect on the group. The ten to twenty minutes of silence each day was also very helpful, though some in the group had to work up to that amount by starting with five minutes, moving to ten and then to fifteen.

These three plans reveal how important balance and moderation are. I hope you will use them as guidelines, and not something to slavishly imitate. Still, there is value in learning—and even imitating for a time—the practices of those who are more experienced than we are. Paul wrote to the Corinthians,

> Though you might have ten thousand guardians in Christ, you do not have many fathers. Indeed, in Christ Jesus I became your father through the gospel. I appeal to you, then, be imitators of me. (1 Corinthians 4:15-16)

Paul told them to imitate him not because he was the perfect model but because he was *the only* model they had. When we start out, it is a good idea to try to do what seasoned apprentices do.

I learned this from my time with Richard Foster and Dallas Willard. In my younger days I imitated their practices. Richard's prayer life was particularly inspiring to me, and I prayed as I saw him pray. I even imitated the way he sat in his chair, with his hands on his knees. When I lived and worked with Dallas Willard, I was impressed with how he memorized the Bible—in large sections. I observed him doing that late into the evening some nights before retiring. I was inspired by this and started doing it myself. But in time I learned to shape and modify what I was doing to fit who I am and what I need. And that changes over time. So I offer these rules and ideas for reflection. Pray about this and consider how you might practice a rule in your own life.

3. LIVING YOUR PLAN IN COMMUNITY

Once you have come up with a balanced and moderate plan, it is time to put it into practice. Simply having a plan will do you no good; you have to live it. This means, first of all, looking over your schedule and planning when you will engage in these practices. This is a crucial step in the process and a place where many fail. They never schedule it, and it never happens. For example, if you are going to have a weekly sabbath, put it in your datebook and plan accordingly. Second, I have found it helpful to keep my plan in front of me as much as possible. Make some copies and put one on your refrigerator and another on your bathroom mirror. Out of sight leads to out of mind. Making your plan visible provides a constant reminder.

Next, find some people who can meet regularly to ask, "How's it going with your plan?" This kind of accountability is of immense value. Studies have shown that people who are accountable increase their ability to achieve goals. You may not need it for the first week or two when your enthusiasm is high, but over time you will need to be accountable to keep going. I also suggest using processing questions to help assess the impact of your plan and to discover where you are struggling and need change. The following questions can be used to help you analyze how God is at work in your spiritual training program.

Examen for Individuals

1. How am I seeing God at work in what I am doing?

2. Which practices am I enjoying the most? The least?

3. What, if anything, needs to be modified or changed in my rule?

Examen for Groups

1. Which old, false narratives have you struggled with since we last met?

2. How are you doing with your rule?

3. What is God teaching you through the practices in your rule?

4. How can we support you?

The following values of an apprentice of Jesus come from The Apprentice Series. They are the kinds of values all followers of Jesus should strive to live up to. A group of apprentices should review this list to see how they are doing personally and as a group.

Values of an Apprentice of Jesus
- noncooperation with wrongdoing
- sensitivity in service to others
- habitual prayer for all people and in all areas of my life
- nonretaliation when others try to harm me
- refusal to be ruled by avarice or sexual desire
- use my resources to invest in heavenly treasures
- refusal to gossip or judge others
- conscious of and conscientiousness toward people in need
- intentionally speak words of encouragement
- labor to do all things well, which glorifies my Father in the heavens

A FINAL WORD OF ENCOURAGEMENT

If you have made it this far—reading all three books and putting these exercises into practice—you have done something pretty special. Having worked on these books for the past ten years and taken over a hundred people through these studies in small group settings, I know how challenging it is. The wonderful thing is that it works. If you are still reading this, I suspect you know it as well. There are so many great books and curricula available to us today—from *Companions in Christ* to *Discipleship Essentials* to *Disciple: Becoming Disciples Through Bible Study*—that we cannot say we lack in resources or ability. The real issue comes down to this: Will we do it? Will we stay the course? Will we keep working on deepening our love for God, taking care of ourselves and loving our neighbor? I pray that you have gained some ideas and practices that will help you as you continue to grow in the grace and knowledge of our Lord Jesus Christ.

appendix

small group discussion guide

BY matthew johnson
with christopher jasen fox

This book has been born from a truth many of us know from our own spiritual journeys: we need community. As this material has been developed it has always been within the context of community. It is within community that we can share the excitement of discovering God's kingdom at work in our lives. It is within community that we can celebrate new insights from this reading material and also challenge the ideas of the author. It is within community that we realize the gifts God has given to us personally and to our brothers and sisters in Christ. It is also within community that we uncover the wounds and issues that the Holy Spirit is bringing to the light.

What a wonderful gift community truly is!

And so, as with the previous books in The Apprentice Series, we have created this small group guide as a tool to help individuals become community. In this guide you will find a session for each chapter. Each session is split into segments. Use these segments in whatever way is most comfortable for your setting. You may skip segments or questions, or you may choose to add questions and activities as you see fit. In addition, you may want to spend time as a group looking at the questions contained within the margins of each chapter.

Depending on the size of your group, the sessions in this guide could take anywhere from sixty to ninety minutes. We have included estimates on how long each segment can take. If your group has more than six participants, expect the group time to last ninety minutes.

If you are the leader of a group, visit The Apprentice Series website at www.apprenticeofjesus.org for a more developed leader's guide for the series as well as podcasts, blogs, videos, other resources and information.

May you be blessed with a loving and peculiar community as you seek God's kingdom in your midst.

Matthew Johnson

CHAPTER 1: THE PECULIAR COMMUNITY

OPENING TO GOD [5 MINUTES]
Begin with five minutes of silence to allow the group to become centered in the present moment and let the busyness and tension of the day drop from their shoulders. At the conclusion of the silence someone in the group may offer a brief prayer, ring a meditation chime or simply say amen.

SOUL TRAINING [10-20 MINUTES]
If you are in a group of six or more people, divide into groups of three or four. Use the questions below to discuss your experience of spend-

ing two hours with God and performing four acts of peculiarity.

Two Hours with God

1. As you are comfortable, share with your group how you spent your two hours with God (in one long block, eight fifteen-minute blocks, one hour of worship?).

2. How did you utilize the author's eight suggested steps for quiet time? If you left any steps out, why did you omit them?

3. What challenges did you encounter in spending two hours with God?

4. How did the time with God affect you?

Four Acts of Peculiarity

1. What effect did your four acts of peculiarity have on you?

2. What challenges did you experience in fulfilling this soul-training exercise?

3. How were your acts of peculiarity an expression of God's peculiarity?

4. Did your "maladjusted" actions ever give you a sense of being a citizen of another world (the kingdom of God)? Describe your experience.

ENGAGING THE CHAPTER [30-40 MINUTES]

If you divided into subgroups for your discussion of the soul-training exercise, you may regroup for your discussion of the chapter. If time is limited, read through the following questions and note which ones you especially want to discuss, and then begin with those questions.

1. What is your earliest recollection of church? How did it shape your understanding of God and of sharing life with others?

2. Can you recall a time you encountered a good and beautiful commu-

nity? If so, describe your experience and what the group was like.

3. Read aloud the Athenagoras quote on pages 28-29. What is most striking to you about his description of the Christians? What would he write about Christians in your community?

4. The author gives us this description of God's peculiar people:

> For example, if I (by the power of the Spirit) begin telling the truth in my life, I will become an oddity. If I can learn to slow down, live without being ruled by anger and actually pray for people who try to cut me down, I will be considered weird. (p. 27)

Then Cornel West gives us this description of how we are to be maladjusted to the ways of the world: "There have always been Christians who are well-adjusted to greed, well-adjusted to fear, well-adjusted to bigotry" (p. 34). The author adds, "All Christians *ought* to be maladjusted to things like injustice, greed, materialism and racism."

- Do you agree that Christians should be "peculiar" and "maladjusted"? Why or why not?

- On page 31 the author writes, "The God that Jesus reveals is peculiar." What is your reaction to this statement?

5. Reread the first four paragraphs of "Trust the Leading of the Spirit" on pages 35-36.

- What wisdom do you draw from George Fox's response to William Penn regarding wearing his sword?

- Is there any area of your life where you wish someone would tell you what to do? How can you apply Fox's principle?

ENGAGING THE WORD [10-20 MINUTES]
Have a volunteer read aloud Romans 12:1-2. Then discuss the following questions.

1. As a group, create a list of words and phrases from this passage

that point to the peculiarity of Christians. Explain why you have chosen those words.

2. What does the phrase "be transformed by the renewing of your minds" mean? How do we do that?

3. Why would the renewing of our minds lead us to not be "conformed to this world"?

GO IN PEACE [5 MINUTES]
Have a volunteer read aloud the following Scripture passage and quote from the book.

> Beloved, let us love one another, because love is from God; everyone who loves is born of God and knows God. Whoever does not love does not know God, for God is love. God's love was revealed among us in this way: God sent his only Son into the world so that we might live through him. In this is love, not that we loved God but that he loved us and sent his Son to be the atoning sacrifice for our sins. Beloved, since God loved us so much, we also ought to love one another. No one has ever seen God; if we love one another, God lives in us, and his love is perfected in us. (1 John 4:7-12)

The ethic is simple: as God is, so should his people be. If we do not love, we must not know God. Because "God's love was revealed among us" in the person of Jesus "that we might live through him" (p. 32).

NEXT WEEK
The next chapter explores the source of hope for the Christian community. The soul-training exercise is sharing your faith. The author gives very constructive steps to make this happen. However, you will need to begin early in the week in order to see the impact of these steps prior to your next gathering.

CHAPTER 2: THE HOPEFUL COMMUNITY

OPENING TO GOD [5 MINUTES]

Begin with five minutes of silence. At the conclusion of the silence someone in the group may offer a brief prayer, ring a meditation chime or simply say amen.

SOUL TRAINING [10-20 MINUTES]

If you are in a group of six or more people, divide into groups of three or four. Use the questions below to discuss your experience of sharing your faith.

1. Have you been practicing any of the seven steps prior to reading this chapter? How does it encourage you to know that you are already playing a significant role in reaching others?

2. Which of the seven activities was most helpful to you? Why?

3. What difficulties did you discover as you worked through these steps? What might these difficulties have to teach you?

4. How will you apply these steps beyond this study?

5. What did you learn about God, yourself or others through this soul-training exercise?

ENGAGING THE CHAPTER [30-40 MINUTES]

If you divided into subgroups for your discussion of the soul-training exercise, you may regroup for your discussion of the chapter. If time is limited, read through the following questions and note which ones you especially want to discuss, and then begin with those questions.

1. What have been your experiences with witnessing, evangelism or faith sharing?

2. Of the six excuses for not witnessing (p. 45), which one are you most inclined to use for not sharing your faith story? Why?

3. John Zizioulas writes that the Christian community "has its roots

in the future and its branches in the present" (p. 48). How does this quote and the author's interpretation of the quote make you feel about the future and the present?

4. Review "The Four-Part Story of Hope" (pp. 48-51). What new or challenging ideas did you find in this section? As you place yourself in this metanarrative, how do you feel?

5. As Christ's story becomes our story, we receive a new identity that forms the foundation for our behavior, but this is not how we normally think. The author explains:

> We almost always do the reverse: we define identity on the basis of behavior; we tell people what they must do (imperative) to find out who they are (indicative). Paul does the opposite: he tells them who they are and then how they should live. The more we grow into the story, the more the story grows into us. (p. 52)

How has your identity in Christ led to changes in behavior?

6. The author points out that our lives are a witness:

> When we tell the truth when it is hard, when we sit in the waiting room with a hurting and scared friend when we have pressing things to do, when we strive to stay in harmony with people who disagree with us, when we find a way to spend less so we can give more, when we offer a blessing to someone who curses at us, the essence of Jesus, who lives in and through us, is emerging. (p. 55)

Spend a few minutes in silent reflection. Think over the last week and consider when the essence of Jesus was emerging in your life or in someone you know. If you are comfortable, share your insights with the group.

7. The author invites us to be prepared to give the reason for the hope we have, gently, respectfully and when the person is ready to

hear it. How does this approach affect your willingness to share your faith?

ENGAGING THE WORD [10-20 MINUTES]

Have a volunteer read the following Scripture aloud. Then discuss the questions.

> We always thank God, the Father of our Lord Jesus Christ, when we pray for you, because we have heard of your faith in Christ Jesus and of the love you have for all the saints—the faith and love that spring from the hope that is stored up for you in heaven and that you have already heard about in the word of truth, the gospel that has come to you. (Colossians 1:3-6 NIV)

1. In your own life, when has hope produced faith and love?

2. If hope is confidence in a good future, how would you describe your level of hope?

3. What truths about God and God's kingdom increase your hopefulness in a good future?

GO IN PEACE [5 MINUTES]

To send you forth, have a volunteer read the following quote from the book.

> Roots in the future, roots in the resurrection, roots in the eternal victory of Jesus, roots that are firmly planted in eternal life, roots that nourish the trunk and the branches, and ultimately produce the fruit that draws others into the story. Wright concludes, "To be truly effective in this kind of mission, one must be genuinely and cheerfully rooted in God's renewal." We have a real reason to cheer. The more we know the story, the more we rejoice. (p. 48)

NEXT WEEK

The next chapter explores the role of self-sacrifice within the Christian community. The soul-training exercise involves self-sacrifice in various areas of our lives.

CHAPTER 3: THE SERVING COMMUNITY

OPENING TO GOD [5 MINUTES]

Begin with five minutes of silence. At the conclusion of the silence someone in the group may offer a brief prayer, ring a meditation chime or simply say amen.

SOUL TRAINING [10-20 MINUTES]

If you are in a group of six or more people, divide into groups of three or four. This chapter's soul-training exercise invited us to live unselfishly in multiple settings. With these questions, work through the different areas where you interact with others.

1. Select two of the following areas and describe what you learned about unselfish living:

   • family

   • work

   • church

   • daily life

2. What was the most difficult aspect of living unselfishly?

3. What did you learn about others as you lived unselfishly?

4. Did you grow in your ability to treasure others through this practice?

ENGAGING THE CHAPTER [30-40 MINUTES]

If you divided into subgroups for your discussion of the soul-training exercise, you may regroup for your discussion of the chapter. If time is limited, read through the following questions and note which ones you especially want to discuss, and then begin with those questions.

1. The author opens the chapter with the story of a committee meeting. How have you seen narratives of self-centeredness and self-sacrifice at work inside or outside the church? What has been the fruit of those meetings?

2. In exploring the false and true narratives, the author contrasts a self-focused church with an others-focused church (pp. 68-70). Consider your own faith community. With your group, list the ways your community is self-focused and others-focused. What do these lists tell you?

3. The author writes, "The value of a church is not in its longevity but in its love. The success of a church is not in its size but in its service to the people and the community" (pp. 72-73). Do churches struggle to focus on love instead of longevity, and service over size? What factors contribute to this struggle?

4. What was your reaction to the author's idea of "treasuring our treasure"? Why?

5. How do you feel about what Dallas Willard says: "The most important task we have, especially for those in church leadership, is to pray for the success of our neighboring churches" (p. 76)?

6. Can you think of a time you gave yourself the "space of grace" (p. 77)? If so, how did the space affect the situation?

ENGAGING THE WORD [10-20 MINUTES]
Have a volunteer read aloud Philippians 2:3-11, then discuss the following questions.

1. What does this passage tell us about the narratives of Jesus?

2. How would you describe the metanarrative of this text (the bigger story)?

3. As a group, create a list of tangible ways you can follow the example of Christ, who humbled himself for the sake of others. Individually consider which items you could do this week.

GO IN PEACE [5 MINUTES]

Have a volunteer read aloud this quote from the book:

Communities become others-centered when they are steeped in the narrative of the kingdom of God. They know that their community is an outpost of the kingdom of God, a place where grace is spoken and lived for as long as is needed. (p. 72)

May our communities become such places.

NEXT WEEK

The next chapter considers what unites a Christian community. The soul-training exercise is expressing love toward those you disagree with. There are practical suggestions for this soul training, but you will need the full week to be able to implement them.

CHAPTER 4: THE CHRIST-CENTERED COMMUNITY

OPENING TO GOD [5 MINUTES]

Begin with five minutes of silence. At the conclusion of the silence someone in the group may offer a brief prayer, ring a meditation chime or simply say amen.

SOUL TRAINING [10-20 MINUTES]

If you are in a group of six or more people, divide into groups of three or four. Use the questions below to discuss your experience of loving those with whom you disagree.

1. What tangible steps did you take to express love toward those you disagree with?

2. How did the interaction change your perspective?

3. Which of John Wesley's five practices seems most difficult? Why do you think this is so?

4. Two additional exercises involved praying for the unity of the church as well as pastors and leaders. As you offered these prayers, how did your focus shift?

ENGAGING THE CHAPTER [30-40 MINUTES]

If you divided into subgroups for your discussion of the soul-training exercise, you may regroup for your discussion of the chapter. If time is limited, read through the following questions and note which ones you especially want to discuss, and then begin with those questions.

1. The author opens this chapter with a story of being rejected by an audience because of his theological terminology. Discuss a time when you have experienced rejection by other Christians. How did that rejection make you feel?

2. The true narrative of this chapter is, "If you do not look, act, worship or believe as I do, but your heart beats in love for Jesus, then regardless of our differences, we can and must have fellowship with one another" (p. 89). What relationships in your life have illustrated this true narrative?

3. On page 93 the author recounts an experience of serving Communion and realizing that many different types of hands were becoming one in the body of Christ. What did you take from this story?

4. Drawing from the wisdom of John Wesley, the author writes, "We can, and will, differ in how we think, which style of worship we prefer, which method of baptism we affirm, but these are not essential. The only thing that matters is that our hearts beat in love for Jesus. If we have that, we are united" (p. 96). How

would the church look different today if people held this belief?

5. Discuss any positive experiences you have had worshiping with people of a different background than your own. How does this affect your openness to future opportunities for such worship?

6. Have a volunteer read aloud the vision written by Richard Foster on pages 101-2, then discuss the following questions.

- What does this passage say about God's vision for the church?

- What does it stir within you? How would you like to respond?

ENGAGING THE WORD [10-20 MINUTES]

For this chapter, the Scripture will be explored using the practice of *lectio divina*. One person in the group will need to serve as the leader, indicating when to move on to the next step. Use the following steps as a group.

- Begin with a few minutes of silence. Then have someone read aloud John 17:20-21 to the group.

  I ask not only on behalf of these, but also on behalf of those who will believe in me through their word, that they may all be one. As you, Father, are in me and I am in you, may they also be in us, so that the world may believe that you have sent me. (John 17:20-21)

- Spend a few minutes allowing the overall scope of these verses to sink into your mind. Reflect on what Jesus is saying in this text.

- Have a different volunteer slowly read the passage a second time. As the passage is read, note any word or phrase that catches your attention. Spend a few minutes in silence, simply meditating on this word or phrase.

- Before the third reading, each person in the group should share the word or phrase that he or she was meditating on during the silence. (Do not give any explanation of the word.)

- Have a third volunteer slowly read the passage again. Following the reading, spend more time in silent dialogue with God, exploring why God has drawn your attention to this word or phrase. Consider what God is inviting you to know or do through this word.

- After the silence, those who are comfortable may share a sentence or two describing what they feel God is inviting them to do.

- Have a fourth volunteer read the passage a final time. Following this reading, enter into a time of silence and simply rest in God's loving presence. After five to ten minutes have a volunteer offer a simple prayer of thanksgiving to God for this time of prayer.

GO IN PEACE [5 MINUTES]

To conclude your time together, have a volunteer read aloud the following quote from the book:

> How can we agree with people who refuse to agree with us? How can we be "united in mind and thought" when clearly we do not agree on every point? Should we simply let go of our ideas, opinions or doctrines? We will never agree on all things, but we can and must agree on one thing: Jesus is Lord. (p. 94)

Amen!

NEXT WEEK

The next chapter explores reconciliation and forgiveness within the Christian community. The soul-training exercise gives three options for practicing forgiveness. As a group look at the three exercises listed on pages 122-24. Is there anyone who would like to practice option one, allowing others to forgive for you? If so, is there a volunteer in the group who would be willing to take on the burden of unforgiveness and begin holding the situation in prayer?

When the group comes together next week you will be able to share your experiences with this practice. The other options can be practiced individually.

CHAPTER 5: THE RECONCILING COMMUNITY

OPENING TO GOD [5 MINUTES]
Begin with five minutes of silence. At the conclusion of the silence someone in the group may offer a brief prayer, ring a meditation chime or simply say amen.

SOUL TRAINING [10-20 MINUTES]
The soul-training exercises involve various steps toward and ways to experience forgiveness. Each of these three questions correlates to the three soul-training exercises; in groups of three or four, answer the questions that apply.

1. If you allowed others to forgive for you, discuss the ways this practice affected you. If you were bearing the burden of unforgiveness for someone, describe your experience of daily prayer and what changed within you.

2. The author gives two steps toward forgiving someone who has hurt you: "identity" and "perspective" (p. 123). If you focused on either of these steps, explore with your group how they helped and what challenges you encountered.

3. The third practice was seeing something new in the Lord's Supper. If you tried this, reflect on what you noticed for the first time in the Lord's Supper and how it relates to forgiveness and reconciliation.

ENGAGING THE CHAPTER [30-40 MINUTES]
If you divided into subgroups for your discussion of the soul-train-

ing exercise, you may regroup for your discussion of the chapter. If time is limited, read through the following questions and note which ones you especially want to discuss, and then begin with those questions.

1. The author begins the chapter with the story of Stan. How did this story make you feel? What role did narratives, community and soul training play in his transformation and healing?

2. The false narrative stated in the chapter is, "Only when we forgive will we be forgiven and healed" (p. 110), but the true narrative is, "Only when we know we have been forgiven will we find healing and become able to forgive" (p. 112). As a group, discuss your comfort or discomfort with these ideas. Reflect on the parts of these narratives that you agree and disagree with.

3. Who do you most identify with in Jesus' story of forgiveness in Matthew 18? Explain.

4. Clarifying that forgiveness is not something we generate from our own willpower, the author explains, "Jesus . . . is both the *pattern* and the *power* of forgiveness and reconciliation" (p. 118). When have you experienced the power of Jesus that allowed you to forgive someone? Discuss this experience with your group.

5. The author recounts his experience of confession with Richard Foster (pp. 118-19). As a group, name your own experiences with confession. When have you experienced deepened trust through the confession of sins and the affirmation of God's forgiveness?

6. Review the two sections titled "Keeping Boundaries of Forgiveness" (pp. 119-20) and "The Forgiveness Ambush" (pp. 120-21). How are these sections helpful? What difficult questions about forgiveness still remain for you?

ENGAGING THE WORD [10-20 MINUTES]

Have a volunteer read aloud the following Scripture passage and quote from the book:

> All this is from God, who reconciled us to himself through Christ, and has given us the ministry of reconciliation; that is, in Christ God was reconciling the world to himself, not counting their trespasses against them, and entrusting the message of reconciliation to us. (2 Corinthians 5:18-19)

In response to this passage the author writes:

> This is a clear explanation of the finality of the cross. God—in Christ—is not counting our sins against us. God stopped counting and apparently never took it back up. God is no longer dealing with us on the basis of our sins but of our faith. Jesus died for all of the sins of all of the people for all time—and that means you. Do you know that? Do you have that peace that passes all understanding? Do you have the joy of knowing that God has nothing against you? (p. 112)

1. As a group, discuss times you have experienced the finality of the cross and the joy that message brings.

2. How has your knowledge of God's forgiveness empowered you to be a minister of reconciliation to others?

GO IN PEACE [5 MINUTES]

Conclude your time by having partners pray for each other to know God's forgiveness and reconciliation in a deeper way.

NEXT WEEK

The next chapter explores encouragement and accountability within the Christian community. The soul-training exercise is meeting with an accountability friend. You will need to work out the details for this meeting early in the week.

CHAPTER 6: THE ENCOURAGING COMMUNITY

OPENING TO GOD [5 MINUTES]

Begin with five minutes of silence. At the conclusion of the silence someone in the group may offer a brief prayer, ring a meditation chime or simply say amen.

SOUL TRAINING [10-20 MINUTES]

If you are in a group of six or more people, divide into groups of three or four. Use the questions below to discuss your experience of meeting with an accountability friend.

1. Were you able to find an accountability friend?

2. How did the time of conversation with this person affect you?

3. Have you had any experiences with an accountability friend (or group) in the past? How would you compare that experience with this week's experience?

4. What resistance do you feel toward having an accountability friend?

ENGAGING THE CHAPTER [30-40 MINUTES]

If you divided into subgroups for your discussion of the soul-training exercise, you may regroup for your discussion of the chapter. If time is limited, read through the following questions and note which ones you especially want to discuss, and then begin with those questions.

1. The author opens the chapter with the story of the Claypot Church and their pastor, Tom Smith. What from that opening section inspired and challenged you?

2. In discussing the false narrative, the author explores how churches lower their expectations and eradicate commitment at the risk of decreasing genuine transformation (pp. 128-29). Describe the level of commitment you have been expected to make in various

churches you've attended. How did the level of commitment affect you? Have you ever seen a higher level of commitment lead to genuine transformation? If so, discuss what you saw.

3. As the author explains the true narrative he writes, "I want a community who reminds me of who I am and will watch over me with love—which means offering both comfort and warning—so that I might live a life worthy of my calling" (pp. 130-31). Do you desire such a community for yourself? What attracts you to this idea, and what reluctance do you feel toward this type of community?

4. On a Sunday morning when the author did not want to go to church, he ended up being reminded of his identity. He writes, "I know who I am: loved, forgiven, cleansed, made alive and destined for eternal joy. As we sing, the community reminds me who I am" (p. 132). Discuss times when your community of faith has reminded you of your identity.

5. Has there been a person or group in your life who has spurred you on to love and good deeds? If so, please describe what happened.

6. The author tells us, "To admonish is to warn, to watch out for and to offer guidance to another" (p. 136). Why do you think we are reluctant to admonish one another? How can these concerns be addressed?

7. Do you agree with Dallas Willard's theory that if we gave good training to the 10 percent of the people in church who are ready and willing to grow, they would grow and their transformation would lead to a change in others? Why or why not?

ENGAGING THE WORD [10-20 MINUTES]

Have a volunteer read aloud 1 Thessalonians 5:14. Notice that there are specific gifts that are offered to people with specific needs, for example, idleness receives warning, and encouragement is given to the timid.

1. Has there ever been a time when someone in your faith community encouraged you? Explain.

2. Have you ever seen someone offer the wrong gift to a person (for example, offering warning to the weak, or patience to the idle)?

3. How do we discern what a person needs as we stand and walk beside them?

4. Give specific examples of situations in which you could practice patience this week.

GO IN PEACE [5 MINUTES]

Have a volunteer from the group read the following quote:

> I want a community who will challenge me to become who I already am: one in whom Christ dwells and delights, a light to the world, salt to the earth, the aroma of Christ to a dying world. I want a community who reminds me of who I am and will watch over me with love—which means offering both comfort and warning—so that I might live a life worthy of my calling. (pp. 130-31)

NEXT WEEK

The next chapter focuses on generosity. The soul-training exercise is applying frugality to your time, treasures and talents in order to create margin to then be more generous.

CHAPTER 7: THE GENEROUS COMMUNITY

OPENING TO GOD [5 MINUTES]

Begin with five minutes of silence. At the conclusion of the silence someone in the group may offer a brief prayer, ring a meditation chime or simply say amen.

SOUL TRAINING [10-20 MINUTES]

If you are in a group of six or more people, divide into groups of three or four. Use the questions below to discuss your experience of applying frugality to your time, talent and treasures so you could then be generous with those resources.

1. What challenges did you experience in being frugal in these three areas?

2. Did you notice an increase in your margin? If so, how?

3. What new ways were you able to be generous as a result of your frugality and increased margin?

4. Does your faith community tend to put more emphasis on the stewardship of time, talents or treasures? How does this emphasis affect your own practices?

5. If you did the additional exercise of writing a paragraph about your generous community, share how your paragraph made you feel.

ENGAGING THE CHAPTER [30-40 MINUTES]

If you divided into subgroups for your discussion of the soul-training exercise, you may regroup for your discussion of the chapter. If time is limited, read through the following questions and note which ones you especially want to discuss, and then begin with those questions.

1. The author begins this chapter by telling the story of his mixed feelings about taking a homeless man to dinner. Discuss your experiences of helping those in need and the feelings these situations produced.

2. There are three false narratives that prevent generosity: "God helps those who help themselves" (p. 149). "If I give it away, I have less" (p. 150), and "What I have is mine to use for my own pleasure" (p. 150). Which of these three false narratives is strongest in your life? Tell the stories of how you came to believe these narratives.

3. In explaining the third true narrative that everything is God's and I am a steward of those resources, the author writes, "We are stewards of God's gifts; everything belongs to God. That changes everything. . . . This fundamental shift affects all of our daily decisions" (p. 153). Spend a few minutes silently reflecting on the daily decisions you make that are affected by this shift. In a journal or in the margin of your book, write what you might do differently because of this knowledge. If you are willing, share your notes with two or three others in your group as a way to hold each other accountable.

4. The author recounts several individuals who share their gifts with him, and he has learned to humbly receive those gifts. Name one or two people who are a profound blessing to you. Are you able to receive their gifts without repaying them? Why or why not?

5. The three ways to become a generous community are (1) learning the joy of giving, (2) practicing margin and (3) learning ways to give (pp. 161-62). Which of these is most lacking in your faith community? How could you increase your knowledge or skill in this area?

6. What is your reaction to the idea that we cannot give from beyond the grave but can give only now? If you agree with this statement, what changes might you make to your daily life?

ENGAGING THE WORD [10-20 MINUTES]
Have a volunteer read aloud 2 Corinthians 8:13-14.

> I do not mean that there should be relief for others and pressure on you, but it is a question of a fair balance between your present abundance and their need, so that their abundance may be for your need, in order that there may be a fair balance. (2 Corinthians 8:13-14)

1. When has someone else's abundance and generosity supplied your want?

2. When has sharing your abundance helped someone else in their need and led to equality?

GO IN PEACE [5 MINUTES]
Have a volunteer read aloud this quote from the book:

A gospel of abundance is found only in the kingdom of God, where somehow we have what we need when we need it. The kingdom of God is not like an ATM where we can get an endless supply of resources to spend however we like. It is a dispenser of resources offered to those who understand the ways of the kingdom. Where there is a need and a person who can meet that need, the supply will never run out. (p. 154)

Let us go out seeking the kingdom!

NEXT WEEK
The next chapter looks at the role of worship in Christian community. The soul-training exercise gives us five steps to prepare for worship.

CHAPTER 8: THE WORSHIPING COMMUNITY

OPENING TO GOD [5 MINUTES]
Begin with five minutes of silence. At the conclusion of the silence someone in the group may offer a brief prayer, ring a meditation chime or simply say amen.

SOUL TRAINING [10-20 MINUTES]
This chapter's soul-training exercise moved us through five steps that prepared us for worship, helped us focus during worship and applied what God was calling us to do following worship. If you are in a group of six or more people, divide into groups of three or four. Use these questions to explore these five steps.

1. Were you able to prepare for worship by creating margin, arriving early and entering with holy expectancy? If so, what impact did these steps have on your worship experience?

2. What one aspect of worship did you focus on this week? What did you notice or learn from this?

3. What one thing did you feel God was inviting you to do? Have you had an opportunity to respond? If so, what has been the result?

ENGAGING THE CHAPTER [30-40 MINUTES]

If you divided into subgroups for your discussion of the soul-training exercise, you may regroup for your discussion of the chapter. If time is limited, read through the following questions and note which ones you especially want to discuss, and then begin with those questions.

1. The author gives us two false and two true narratives (pp. 170-73). Which of the false narratives is most at work in your life? How can you tell? Do you agree with the true narratives? Why?

2. In summarizing the quote from C. S. Lewis, the author writes, "We need each other, despite our differences. And worship is not about the quality of the performance but the heart of those who worship" (p. 174). How have differences within your worshiping community been a blessing to you? How would you describe the heart of your worshiping community?

3. In his letter to his son, Jacob, the author explains the value and importance of several elements of worship. What did you find most helpful from this section (pp. 177-84)? Why?

4. If you are comfortable, discuss your struggles with worship—the hurt, disappointment, disillusionment or burnout that has made worship difficult for you. Conclude this time of sharing with prayer for one another and for anyone struggling to find a worship home.

5. In our current culture it is easy to become a worship consumer. What are the indications that you are more focused on critiquing worship than you are on critiquing your own heart?

6. Read the quote from *Jayber Crow* on pages 184-85. What emotions does this story stir within you? How does it change your perspective of worship, your faith community and your place in that community?

ENGAGING THE WORD [10-20 MINUTES]

Have a volunteer read aloud Psalm 95:1-3.

1. When you read this psalm, does it encourage or discourage you regarding your own worship experience? Why?

2. Why do we feel our worship experience needs to match the psalmist's?

3. Have you ever felt the type of joy in worship David is describing? Recount your experience.

4. David's narrative in the psalm is that God is a rock, Lord and King above all gods. What connection is there between David's view of the good and beautiful God and his response in worship?

GO IN PEACE [5 MINUTES]

Have a volunteer read the following quote aloud as a benediction for your time together:

> Christianity is not a religion but the formation of a people through the gospel—the good news that God in Christ has reconciled the world. Religion is the human search for God; Christianity is God's search for humans. We do not worship so much as we respond. "Through Christ in the Spirit we respond to the Father's love. This is the ground-pattern of Christian worship." (p. 173)

NEXT WEEK

The final section of the book gives guidance for creating a soul-shaping plan. The next session will give the group a chance to reflect on their soul-training plans and possibly create a soul-shaping plan for the entire group.

CHAPTER 9: WRITING A SOUL-TRAINING PLAN

This session is intended to help groups process their experience with the individual rule as well as provide guidance for creating a group rule.

OPENING TO GOD

Begin with five minutes of silence followed by a short prayer of thanksgiving for the journey your group has shared.

ENGAGING THE CHAPTER

Utilize the following questions to explore the process of creating your individual rule and learn from others in the group.

1. Discuss your process for picking the soul-training exercises that form the basis for your rule. What was easy and what was difficult about creating that list?

2. The second step in creating a soul-training strategy is adding practices that are not part of The Apprentice Series. What other practices did you add to the list? Did any of your additions surprise you?

3. When you first looked at your list of spiritual disciplines, was there any imbalance? Did you have to cut back on anything to make it sustainable?

4. As you followed your rule this week, how did it affect your relationship with God?

5. How would you describe your daily and weekly interactions with

God prior to writing your rule? What was nourishing and what was difficult about your spiritual journey? How does your rule fit into these strengths and weaknesses?

As a group you will need to decide if you will follow the author's suggestion and create a group rule. It may be helpful to clarify that the group will not necessarily be gathered together to observe each of the spiritual practices that make up the group rule. Here are some steps to follow and points to consider if you decide to create such a rule.

1. On slips of paper have each person in the group write down one discipline from their list that is especially meaningful to them. They might also consider if it would be helpful to have others engaging in this discipline at the same time.

2. Compile a list of disciplines from the slips of paper.

3. Decide how often each discipline will be observed. Allow for grace in this matter. One person might have a schedule that allows for two hours of silence each day, but someone else might struggle to have five minutes. Design the rule to support the person who struggles with any discipline. Those who are able to do more can certainly do so on their own.

4. Once the list is complete, check for balance and sustainability. Is anything clearly missing? Is there a good balance between disciplines that relate to God, self and neighbor? Make any necessary adjustments.

5. Each member of the group should write down the rule and the schedule for its observation. It may also be helpful for members to write the rule on a notecard so they can carry it with them.

Other considerations:

- Decide when to meet again to encourage and support one another. (It may be two to four weeks.)

- Make sure you have other ways to be in contact with one another between your gatherings, whether this is through email, a blog or something else. Use this communication to not only discuss the disciplines but also share prayer requests and insights of how God is working in your life.

FUTURE GATHERINGS

Use this suggested outline when the group gathers to reflect on the rule and how God is at work in their lives.

Opening to God

Begin with five minutes of silence followed by an opening prayer, ringing a meditation chime or simply saying amen.

Questions of Examen for Groups

1. Which old, false narratives have you struggled with since we last met?

2. What true narratives have become stronger or clearer since the last meeting?

3. How are you doing with your rule?

4. What is God teaching you through the practices in your rule?

5. How can the group support and encourage you?

Review

Review the group rule and remove disciplines that do not seem connected with your journey as a group (remember, individuals can still observe these practices). Are there any disciplines that should be added? Formalize this new rule and use it until you meet again.

Go in Peace

Conclude your time by reading a Scripture passage or helpful quote or reciting the Lord's Prayer.

Notes

Introduction

p. 15   "splendid, never-to-be-duplicated story of grace": Eugene Peterson, *Living the Message: Daily Help for Living the God-Centered Life* (San Francisco: HarperSanFrancisco, 1996), p. 5. One of my fellow apprentices, Denise Steinacker, first pointed me to this reference.

pp. 16-17   "The awareness of my connection with Jesus": Tony Campolo, quoted from a talk Tony gave in a chapel at Friends University on January 28, 2010.

Chapter 1: The Peculiar Community

pp. 28-29   "The difference between Christians and the rest of mankind": Attributed to Athenagoras, *Epistle to Diognetus*, in *Early Christian Writings* (London: Penguin, 1968), pp. 244-45.

p. 30   Figure 1.1: Rodney Stark, *The Rise of Christianity* (San Francisco: Harper-One, 1996), p. 7. I refer to Mr. Stark as a "secular" historian because at the time of the writing of this book, he was not a practicing Christian. I was recently informed that this has changed. I say "secular" because too often the statistics offered by Christians are suspect. Noting that he was not coming from a faith position helps to show that he was not padding the numbers.

p. 34   "There have always been Christians": Cornel West, on *Bill Moyers Journal*, July 3, 2009. Dr. West appeared alongside two other professors and discussed the theological implications of the financial collapse of 2008-2009.

p. 34   "It takes courage to ask": Cornel West, *Hope on a Tightrope* (New York: Smiley, 2008), pp. 9-10.

Chapter 2: The Hopeful Community

p. 47   "The solid facts about the future hope of Christians": N. T. Wright, *Colossians and Philemon*, Tyndale New Testament Commentary (Downers Grove, Ill.: InterVarsity Press, 1986), p. 56.

p. 48   "has its roots in the future and its branches in the present": John D. Zizioulas, *Being as Communion* (Crestwood, N.Y.: St. Vladimir's Seminary Press, 1977), p. 59.

p. 48   "a mission-shaped church must have its mission shaped by hope": N. T.
               Wright, *Surprised by Hope* (San Francisco: HarperOne, 2008), pp. 269-70.
p. 48   "To be truly effective in this kind of mission": Ibid., p. 270.
p. 51   "The victory of God in our time over this deathly idolatry": Walter Brueg-
               gemann, *Biblical Perspectives on Evangelism* (Nashville: Abingdon, 1993),
               p. 41.
p. 52   "My wholeness, my integrity, is made possible": Stanley Hauerwas, *The
               Peaceable Kingdom* (Notre Dame, Ind.: University of Notre Dame Press,
               1983), p. 94.
pp. 52-53   "The question 'What ought I to be?' ": Ibid., p. 116.
p. 62   average time between seeking and commitment: This comes from a study
               done by Tom Albin of the early Methodists. Albin studied the time frame
               in which the people first came to a Methodist gathering (awakened obvi-
               ously to a need for a deeper life with God) and the date when they experi-
               enced "conversion." The average span of time between first inquiry and
               conversion was twenty-eight months. See Scott J. Jones, *The Evangelistic
               Love of God and Neighbor* (Nashville: Abingdon, 2003), p. 90. The original
               source is Tom Albin, "An Empirical Study of Early Methodist Spirituality,"
               in *Wesleyan Theology Today: A Bicentennial Theological Consultation*, ed.
               Theodore Runyan (Nashville: Kingswood Books, 1985), p. 278.

Chapter 3: The Serving Community
p. 72   "splendid, never-to-be-duplicated stories of grace": Eugene Peterson, *Liv-
               ing the Message: Daily Help for Living the God-Centered Life* (San Francisco:
               HarperSanFrancisco, 2007), p. 5.
p. 74   "O God, help me believe the truth about myself": Macrina Wiederkehr,
               Seasons of Your Heart (San Francisco: HarperOne, 1991), p. 71.

Chapter 4: The Christ-Centered Community
p. 88   "This love that is characteristic of God's kingdom": Stanley Hauerwas, *The
               Peaceable Kingdom* (Notre Dame, Ind.: University of Notre Dame Press,
               1983), p. 91.
p. 90   the Apostles' Creed and the Nicene Creed: The two most commonly used
               creeds in the church are the Apostles' Creed and the Nicene Creed. They
               were composed by church leaders in the early centuries in an effort to
               define the basic beliefs of Christians.
p. 94   "In essentials, unity; in doubtful matters, liberty; in all things, charity":
               Scholars disagree on the origin of this phrase and its author. The phrase
               was originally stated in Latin as: "In necessariis unitas, in non-necessariis
               [or, dubiis] libertas, in utrisque (or, omnibus) caritas."
p. 99   "God's very reality is radically multiple": Serene Jones, quoted in Miroslav
               Volf, *Exclusion and Embrace* (Nashville: Abingdon, 1996), p. 176.
p. 100   "These distinctions . . . have become irrelevant in Christ": N. T. Wright,

Colossians and Philemon, Tyndale New Testament Commentary (Downers Grove, Ill.: InterVarsity Press, 1986), p. 144.

pp. 101-2   "Right now we largely remain": Richard J. Foster, *Streams of Living Water* (San Francisco: HarperSanFrancisco, 1998), pp. 273-74.

p. 103   Wesley's five ways to show love: John Wesley, "The Catholic Spirit," sermon 39. Available at <www.ccel.org/w/wesley/sermons/sermons-html/serm-039.html>.

Chapter 5: The Reconciling Community

p. 105   Stan was a former student of mine: The story about Stan was first told in a book I wrote in 1995 called *Embracing the Love of God*. Then, as now, Stan gave me permission—even encouragement—to tell his story. The reason I am retelling it is twofold: First, it took me many years to understand this story, and only now, with an awareness of the importance of narrative, exercise and community, am I able to understand how Stan was transformed. Second, some things have happened since those days that further enhance the power of his story, and I want to share them with others.

p. 112   a clear explanation of the finality of the cross: I am indebted to author and radio teacher Bob George for this phrase. If he got it from somewhere else, I am not aware of it. Bob was the first person to explain this concept to me with great clarity and with great benefit to my soul.

p. 114   Ten thousand talents is approximately *six hundred thousand times more*: R. T. France, *The Gospel of Matthew*, New International Commentary on the New Testament (Grand Rapids: Eerdmans, 2007), p. 707.

p. 116   "Woe unto you if you try to stand on your rights": Joachim Jeremias, *The Parables of Jesus* (Upper Saddle River, N.J.: Prentice-Hall, 1963), p. 213.

p. 117   "The pattern of our forgiven-ness": L. Gregory Jones, *Embodying Forgiveness* (Grand Rapids: Eerdmans, 1995), p. 166.

p. 117   "Paul here makes two points": N. T. Wright, *Colossians and Philemon*, Tyndale New Testament Commentary (Downers Grove, Ill.: InterVarsity Press, 1986), p. 147.

p. 118   "Christ forgives through us": Miroslav Volf, *Free of Charge: Giving and Forgiving in a Culture Stripped of Grace* (Grand Rapids: Zondervan, 2005), p. 200.

p. 124   "Christ's sacrifice relocates our lives as forgiven betrayers": Jones, *Embodying Forgiveness*, p. 176.

Chapter 6: The Encouraging Community

pp. 126-27   information about Claypot: The story can be found at www.claypot.co.za.

p. 131   "Blessed assurance, Jesus is mine!": Fanny J. Crosby, "Blessed Assurance" (1873).

p. 132   "The Christian needs another Christian": Dietrich Bonhoeffer, *Life Together* (New York: Harper & Row, 1954), p. 23.

p. 139   "I was more convinced than ever": John Wesley, *The Works of John Wesley,* vol. 21, *Journal and Diaries IV,* ed. Reginald Ward and Richard Heitzenrater (Nashville: Abingdon, 1992), p. 424.

Chapter 7: The Generous Community

pp. 153-54   "Generosity is 'other-centered,' whereas greed is self-centered": Matt Johnson, personal communication with the author, fall 2009. Matt is a pastor in Wichita, Kansas, who works with me in the Apprentice ministry.

p. 154   "The idealization of poverty *is one of the most dangerous illusions*": Dallas Willard, *The Spirit of the Disciplines* (San Francisco: Harper & Row, 1988), pp. 194, 199.

p. 154   "We need a third way": Shane Claiborne, quoted in *School(s) for Conversion: 12 Marks of a New Monasticism,* ed. the Rutba House (Eugene, Ore.: Cascade Books, 2005), p. 32.

p. 155   *Forbes* on living well: see David Wann, *Simple Prosperity* (New York: St. Martin's Griffin, 2007), p. 61.

p. 159   "the service of being served": Richard Foster, *Celebration of Discipline* (San Francisco: Harper & Row, 1978), p. 119.

p. 162   "Practicing frugality means we stay within the bounds": Willard, *Spirit of the Disciplines,* p. 168.

p. 164   our time to be generous is limited: I believe we will be able to be generous in heaven. I do not believe there will be money in heaven, for example, but we will have time, and I suspect we will be our unique selves, which can be a blessing to others. The point is that the way we give of our resources on earth will come to an end, thus making it more important to give while we can.

Chapter 8: The Worshiping Community

p. 173   "Through Christ in the Spirit we respond": J. D. Crichton, "A Theology of Worship," in *The Study of Liturgy,* ed. Cheslyn Jones et al. (London: Oxford University Press, 1992), p. 11.

p. 173   "When I first became a Christian, about fourteen years ago": C. S. Lewis, *Letters of C. S. Lewis,* ed. W. H. Lewis (New York: Harcourt Brace Jovanovich, 1966), p. 224.

p. 174   not about "individual fulfillment" but the "constitution of a people": James K. A. Smith, *Desiring the Kingdom* (Grand Rapids: Baker Academic, 2009), p. 153.

pp. 184-85   "One day when I went up there": Wendell Berry, *Jayber Crow* (New York: Counterpoint, 2000), pp. 164-65.

p. 186   "holy expectancy": Richard J. Foster, *Celebration of Discipline* (San Francisco: Harper & Row, 1978), p. 140.

p. 187   "Enter the service ten minutes early": Ibid., p. 142.

p. 188   "Just as worship begins in holy expectancy": Ibid., p. 148.

Acknowledgments

This book—and all of the books in The Apprentice Series—would not exist were it not for Dallas Willard, a living example of a true apprentice of Jesus who has inspired me in countless ways. Dallas's outline of a "curriculum for Christlikeness" is the framework of these books. It is difficult to measure the impact of his life and writings on my soul.

And these books would not have been written if it were not for Richard J. Foster, who has poured his life and wisdom into me for over twenty-five years. Everyone should have a teacher as brilliant and authentic as Richard—I am grateful. Thank you, Richard, for finding something in me worth believing in and taking a chance on.

The person who made the most sacrifice is my wonderful, beautiful, fun and very patient wife, Meghan Smith. She endured many months as a "writer's widow" and never complained. Thank you, Meghan, for knowing how important this series is to me by supporting and encouraging me every step of the way. And thanks for editing the material along the way. My whole life is better because of you. You still take my breath away.

My son and daughter, Jacob and Hope, also gave up a lot as I wrote.

Thank you for allowing me to tell your stories. Thanks too for supporting me while I wrote, rewrote, edited and taught this material. I know that time spent with others is time taken from you. I will work to make it up to you!

I also want to thank my four former disciples and now colleagues for all the encouragement and support you have given me. Thanks to the two "sons of thunder": Patrick Sehl, for your relentless support of me and love for this material; and C. J. Fox, for being an example of integrity and enthusiasm. And to the two wise hobbits: Matt Johnson, for your quiet confidence, dedication to the King and the kingdom, and scent of patchouli; and Jimmy Taylor, for your creativity and depth and sheer love of Jesus. These four young men are going to change the world.

I also want to thank two of my colleagues at Friends University who read the manuscripts of The Apprentice Series, offered a lot of helpful suggestions and helped me avoid some errors—Dr. Stan Harstine for your biblical brilliance, and Dr. Darcy Zabel for your literary skills.

I owe a great debt to Kathy Helmers, my agent and guide through the maze of publishing, for sharing my love for these books, shaping them into something good and then finding the right publishing partner. Kathy, you are the best at what you do, and I am fortunate to work with you.

Thanks to Jeff Crosby and Cindy Bunch of InterVarsity Press, who made it clear to me from the moment we met that you are quality people with incredible skills, a passion for publishing good books, and a clear vision for what this series is and can be. I am blessed to work with you both.

Also, I want to thank Andrew Tash for writing the excellent "box" questions that are in each chapter.

I also need to thank others who contributed in hidden ways:

Bob Casper—for your belief in me and these books and your brilliant mind.

Jeff Gannon—my pastor, friend and fellow worker in the kingdom.

Lyle SmithGraybeal—for never once doubting these books.

Vicki and Scott Price—for loving me and believing in these books.

Ashley Brockus—for encouragement and assistance so the work could get done.

Also, thank you to the people and pastors of Chapel Hill United Methodist Church, Wichita, who studied and practiced the concepts in these books, and allowed me to learn from your experiences and insights. Your presence flows in the pages of these books.

Finally, I want to thank Warren Farha of Eighth Day Books for helping me find just the right books to read and study. There is no better "book person" in this world, and no finer bookstore.

THE
APPRENTICE
SERIES

The Good and Beautiful God
The Good and Beautiful Life
The Good and Beautiful Community

AN
APPRENTICE
RESOURCE

For more information and resources visit
www.apprenticeinstitute.org

APPRENTICE INSTITUTE™
for Christian Spiritual Formation

Under the leadership of James Bryan Smith, The Apprentice Institute (est. 2009), located at Friends University in Wichita, Kansas, provides educational experiences in the area of Christian spirituality, develops resources for individual and church renewal, and engages in research to advance the field of Christian formation.

VISION
The vision of the Apprentice Institute is the renewal of the world and the church through the formation of new people and new communities who have begun living a radical Christian life in conformity to the teachings of Jesus, as his apprentices, in the midst of the world, whether in secular or ministry positions.

PROGRAMS AND EVENTS
The following programs aid in keeping with the Apprentice Institute vision and mission:

- An undergraduate (B.A.) degree in Christian spiritual formation equipping young people to live out their faith as a follower of Jesus no matter their field of study
- A Master of Arts in Christian spiritual formation and leadership designed as a personal growth, academic and professional program (online and residency degree)
- A certificate program, titled Apprentice Experience, is a journey in discipleship intended for anyone wanting to further their study of Christian spiritual formation
- Annual national conference on Christian spiritual formation engaging leaders in the field of Christian spiritual formation

Begin—or extend—your journey of living as an apprentice of Jesus today.

For more information, go to www.apprenticeinstitute.org or email us at info@apprenticeinstitute.org.

FRIENDS
UNIVERSITY